FIERCE GRACE

FIERCE GRACE

LEARNING I'M ENOUGH THROUGH LOVE, LOSS, AND LETTING GO

Rev. Karen L. Weiss

Centre Hall, Pennsylvania

Fierce Grace
Learning I'm enough through love, loss, and letting go

Publisher's Note: Some names and identifying details have been changed to protect the privacy of individuals mentioned in this work.

Requests for information can be sent to Waterworks Ministries through www.waterworksministries.org.

ISBN (ebook): 978-1-7339261-0-2
ISBN (soft cover): 978-1-7339261-1-9

Cover Art: Karen L. Weiss
Cover Design: Lisa Delay, lisadelay.com
Back cover photo credit: Katherine Sleadd, @katesleadd
Developmental and Copy Editing: Ed Cyzewski, edcyzewski.com

Contents

Chapter 1

Introduction

Fierce grace isn't a phrase I considered before 2018. I used to describe grace as gentle, compassionate, and soft and cuddly like a teddy bear. It didn't occur to me that God's grace might be fierce, until this phrase popped into my head while I was washing dishes on New Year's Eve 2017. I was disturbed. But oh, how these words profoundly resonated within my soul!

When I hear the word "fierce," I think of someone who is strong, powerful, focused, commanding, and unwilling to put up with anyone else's crap. A fierce person shows an exceptional, almost over the top intensity of feeling. I would not regularly attribute the characteristic "fierce" to God. God is my friend, my companion, my BFF. I hadn't experienced God as fierce, or so I thought at the time.

When I think of grace, "unmerited favor" immediately comes to mind. We receive it from God, we extend it to each other and to ourselves, and we share it with creation. Theoretically, it's not something from which we can escape if God is giving it to us, yet I repeatedly choose to distance myself from it.

Putting "fierce" and "grace" together gives these words a completely different spin. Fierce grace is God's persistent, relentless, doggedly purposeful, and unyielding (in the most loving way possible) grace-filled presence in our lives. Fierce grace's purpose is to passionately and lovingly nudge us to let go of our stuff—whether emotional, spiritual, relational, mental, or physical— so that we gain greater spiritual freedom and an ever-increasing capacity to love ourselves, God, and the world. Fierce grace is laser-focused on our spiritual transformation and uses whatever means are at her disposal to affect this transformation within us.

One of the main ways fierce grace has transformed me is through spiritual direction. I didn't know what spiritual direction was until my third semester in seminary. I was in the spiritual formation program and "Intro to Spiritual Direction" was one of the required classes. During the Fall 2009 course, I learned that spiritual direction is a conversation between the director, the directee, and the Holy Spirit, generally held monthly for about an hour. Direction is a safe place where the directee can explore how and where God is at work in her life. In addition to holding space for the directee, the director helps the directee notice God's invitations and decide how to respond to them. One of the many things I appreciate about spiritual direction is that nothing is off limits. No topic is too uncomfortable or taboo to discuss with God since God is with us in the shadows as well as the light. Spiritual direction can assist with discernment, finding God in suffering, exploring dreams, and growing in Christ through letting go of false ideologies and dishonoring behavior patterns.

The spiritual direction relationship is a transformative relationship that expands our capacity to love ourselves, others, and creation all while growing closer to God. It's one of the least talked about spiritual disciplines and can be one of the most transformative if we give ourselves to it whole-heartedly. The more I learned in this intro class, the more I was intrigued and afraid. Intrigued because it sounded like something that would help me grow, transform, and be a better person. I was afraid because it would be something that would help me grow, transform, and be a better person! I knew that if I started direction, I'd be forced to confront my obsessive control and self-reliance issues, my desire to be right at all costs, and a whole host of other character and behavioral flaws that I wanted to hang on to.

It took me a year to muster up the courage to seek out the professor from that class and ask her if she was accepting new directees. She was, and I started with Mindy in September 2010. Within three months God put her skills to work in revealing some of my deeply held beliefs that were holding me back from treating myself (and others) with honor and dignity. I still meet with Mindy monthly, and I guard these times as sacred spaces. Nothing gets in my way of meeting with her. Because of my commitment to spiritual direction, prayer, and self-discovery over the last several years, I've allowed fierce grace—although I didn't identify her as "fierce" until 2018—to transform me from the inside out, and the spiritual director in me wants that for you, the reader.

In addition to the main theme of fierce grace, other threads weave through this book: letting go of control and learning to honor myself (and others) by treating myself (and others) with dignity. I'm not sure about you, but I can't control situations and simultaneously treat myself and others with dignity. The two are mutually exclusive in my life. When I am focused on controlling things, what I'm really looking for is certainty amidst the chaos and unknown. I want certainty about ideas, situations, procedures, and my environment. It allows me to feel like I've got it all together, that I know what's up, and, that I'm better than other people more often than I'd like to admit. When I think I'm in control, my perception of order and rightness can maintain a false sense of security and superiority.

In contrast to attempting to control, honoring myself has included lots of messy and chaotic things like tears, overwhelming emotions, leaving behind narratives that don't fit anymore, and evaluating what I believe and why I believe it. Honoring myself and others includes how I treat myself (mind, body, and heart) and how I respond to others. It means that I accept myself as enough, even when I've messed up or done something wrong. Honoring is hard work, and gratefully, it's slowly becoming a habit. Today, I say with hope that I am becoming who God wants me to be; a person who sees herself as a beautiful (and messy) child of God, a woman who honors herself as a woman who has gifts and graces to share with the world. Honoring myself lets me see myself as enough.

As much as we would prefer otherwise, we don't typically grow in God when everything is daisies and sunshine. Frequently, suffering is the starting point for our transformation. Because of this, fierce grace often fulfills her purpose and is most noticeable when we are uncomfortable, suffering, or in a state of dis-ease. She is present and active when we allow ourselves to honor and hold loosely what we've been given; whether it is resources, knowledge, expectations, pain, suffering, or loss. Through discomfort, fierce grace helps us notice the invitations to spiritual transformation and then encourages us to consciously choose our responses. For me, transformation usually happens with repeated invitations to be less controlling and self-reliant and more honoring and trusting. For all of us, transformation occurs when God opens us up to the work of fierce grace through experiencing dis-ease, which includes grief, disappointment, frustration, religious deconstruction, and identity crises, just to name a few.

This book is as much about process as it is about transformation. I would not be the person I am today (and still growing in Christ) without experiencing fierce grace throughout many different aspects of life. I've intentionally shared stories of how fierce grace has shown up to me in the last decade and how she has helped me transform into a more whole and healed individual. To me, the process of transformation is just as important as the result of fierce grace's work in us.

I believe that all of us are being pursued by fierce grace for healing and wholeness. As you read this book, I hope you will identify and reflect on your own journey of transformation. I also hope that you will be encouraged to explore your understanding of God, the limits you might place on God and yourself, as well as live more fully into the person you've been created to be and honor your journey in the process.

Chapter 2

Cracked

Cracked wide open,
    exposing the flesh within.
Wisdom wants in
    For love, dignity, grace.
Yet I run.
    Believing that once I escape
        I will be safe.
"No!" my heart whispers.

"Haven't you learned?
  The safety is in Surrender,
    Allowing Fierce Grace
        To break you,
        To expose
          That which you must keep hidden."

Cracked like a nut
    Against my will (or so it seems).
Exposed. Vulnerable. Afraid.

"Surrender" Wisdom calls.
    "Let me in, I love you!"

Resistance. Fear. Denial.
    Bitterness.
        Grief.
            Resentment.
Mighty foes to Grace?

Against all opposition she cries with glee,
    "You'll see! The prize is
        Worth the terror-tory ahead."

Silence.

"Don't you want to be free?"
    She asks, sadly.
        Forlornly.
"Maybe, but not today." I reply.
    "Not like this."

And yet she stays.
Fierce in her determination
    To love, to pursue me for richness
        I cannot fathom.
Fierce in her yearning for surrender, love, and grace.

Chapter 3

Honoring the Pain

Hindsight is clear that fierce grace has shown up throughout my life. I might not have called it fierce grace, but God's persistent poking and prodding, especially in the last eleven years, hasn't gone unnoticed. If fierce grace is all about transformation, getting me to pay attention what it takes to grow emotionally and spiritually is a big part of fierce grace's pursuit. Right from the beginning of 2018 I noticed that fierce grace was suggesting I pay attention to how (begrudgingly) I've honored my feelings. I'm fairly certain that for most of my life I've not even acknowledged my emotional baggage let alone treat it with dignity.

Fierce grace most definitely shows up in how we honor emotions like grief, sorrow, and loss. For me, this idea raises several questions. Am I willing to face all that I feel or carry with me? Am I willing to hold and experience my grief with dignity and honor? Am I willing to let it crack me open in a way that exposes those deepest parts of me that I don't want anyone, even God or myself for that matter, to know about? Am I willing to let God into those deepest places of anguish so that we can work through it together? Am I willing to let God into those deepest places of anguish so that I can experience fierce grace? More often than not, my first answer is no, with a side of maybe.

My bunny Shaquille died in late-January 2018. She developed a cranky gut over the past year and this time we couldn't save her. The vet believed she had a bowel blockage and told me (at 4:30 am on a frosty January Saturday) that if they didn't do surgery her stomach could rupture and that would be a horrible way to die. My husband Pat was away on a fishing trip and had turned off his phone out of habit when he went to sleep. I had to make the decision alone to say yes to surgery. Unfortunately for me and Pat, Shaq had undergone too much stress since Thursday evening and the anesthesia overwhelmed her. She went into respiratory arrest and could not be resuscitated. We were, and still are, heartbroken. As I write these words tears come to my eyes. Tears well up and spill down my cheeks because I felt it was my duty to protect this sweet, opinionated, and skittish three plus pound ball of fur that we had been given, and I couldn't save her. My heart still breaks as I think about that cold Saturday morning, being all alone and staring into the abyss of grief and loss that took my breath away and has since left a chill in my bones.

I am grateful that I have friends and family who rearranged their schedules so either I could go to them or they could come to me until Pat got back from his trip. They were fierce grace in action, and in significant ways they helped me honor my grief in those first days while I was incapable of holding it intentionally. I spent Sunday morning with a friend having brunch. I cried, was hugged, and had three crazy dogs love on me for a couple hours. Then my parents came and stayed with me through Monday morning. The living room was Shaquille's domain, and it was really hard to sit in there and watch TV with my parents. They noticed and commented on my physical inability to cross the threshold between the kitchen and the living room. They noticed and commented that when I did enter the living room, I couldn't sit down. By the time my parents arrived on Sunday afternoon, I had removed all of Shaq's stuff and moved the furniture so that the Shaq zone wasn't so obvious. I would have completely rearranged the room if there would have been another cable outlet for us to use, but the option wasn't there. So instead of hanging out in the living room all night, we played a few games of Sequence, and I went to bed early. I hadn't gotten a lot of sleep in the last forty-eight hours. And since I couldn't bring myself to sleep on the couch (I had given my parents our bed), I slept in my sleeping bag in my prayer room.

My parents left late Monday morning, and I went to my temp job. I couldn't stand being in the house alone all day. Then Pat returned home on Monday night. We cried together as we stood in the living room holding on to one another. Like so many other pet parents, the loss of a fur-child leaves an indelible mark. She was our baby, and now we have a Shaq-sized hole in our hearts.

Cracked Like a Nut

In learning to honor our emotions, fierce grace shows up in our pain and struggle to nudge us along. As the weeks and months have passed, I've noticed that my grief wells up and overflows in fits and spurts, but especially when I'm writing about her. For me the question of whether I'm willing to let myself be cracked open so that I can grow because of fierce grace is a compelling one. To be cracked open, like a nut or to have open heart surgery. These are different ideas with the same message and potentially the same sound. It's the sound, the "CRACK" that has my attention. The sharp "crack" of a walnut shell breaking open or the breaking of the sternum to allow a surgeon to fix a heart. I've not ever heard a sternum crack but my imagination does the work for me in this instance.

A shell has to be forcefully broken open so that the reward can be enjoyed in the case of the walnut, or that healing or repair of the heart can take place. It takes work to crack open a walnut shell, and I'm not very good at it. It usually takes me a couple tries, with the walnut shooting off sideways and mocking my effort to get at the tasty goodness inside. You have to put the walnut shell in the hand cracker at just the right position and angle so that it breaks easily and doesn't go flying across the room as a projectile. But finding this spot takes practice and persistence. Removing nuts from their shells takes dedication and work for me. There's a discernable goal, of getting at what's inside this hard and thick exterior shell that seems to be so intentionally and stubbornly protecting its interior. It's like the tree said, "Ok, you might REALLY like walnuts, but I'm going to make it difficult for you. You need to show me that you're willing to put in the work to get what's inside, that you REALLY want it." Obviously this metaphor of the spiritual journey only goes so far, but there's something deeply resonant with me in terms of being the walnut, shell and all, and of me being open to brokenness so that I may experience fierce grace.

Simultaneously, I fear that if I crack open, exposing those dark shadows of grief and pain to the light, all I will find will be rotten walnut meat, with maggots, worms, or something gross that will make the walnut inedible so that the experience will be deeply disappointing and potentially humiliating. I'm continually afraid of cracking open and finding rot instead of surprising beauty. It's quite fascinating, to me anyway, how I know (with my head) that in all of my prayer and conversation with Jesus, he never chastises me or displays anger or bitterness at my inability to be whole of my own volition. I know that Jesus wants to love me into complete healing and wholeness (the Hebrew word *shalom* comes to mind) and that all he does is reflective of that desire. I know that in order to be made whole, I actually have to respond affirmatively to the invitations to look at what is broken or isn't put together, that there's an acknowledgement of things to be fixed, pruned, or rebuilt in some way.

These invitations to wholeness are fierce grace in action. I know this. And yet, there's this part of me that is repeatedly terrified of exposing those darkest places to the light. For the first thirty years of my life, I generally ignored my emotions because I was afraid of them overtaking me. I was afraid of being crushed under their weight in such a way that I would be irreparably broken. And to add to the mess, I've been disturbingly afraid of being told that my feelings, pain, grief, actions, and my entire being are wrong.

The Dungeon

Although the words "fierce grace" popped into my head at the beginning of 2018, reflecting on my journey reveals that fierce grace's fingerprints are all over my life and how I honor my emotions and take care of my heart. While in seminary (several years ago) I began working with my spiritual director around this issue of being reluctantly open to experience my emotions and honor my heart. During one particular direction session with Mindy, she suggested that Jesus might have something to tell me regarding my fear of emotion. Mindy asked if I was receptive to spending some time in silent conversation with God, and I agreed.

I am a very visual person, and often when I pray I get mental pictures of scenes and situations that bring the prayer issue into focus. At Mindy's nudge to pray silently about my resistance, I closed my eyes and it was like a movie immediately started on the inside of my eyelids. I was walking with Jesus, and we were in this medieval castle that had a dungeon in the basement. Somehow we ended up in the dungeon because that's where I was keeping my heart. The dungeon was like a suburban cul-de-sac, with a hallway that led to this round room with doors to six cells. The place was dark and damp; it echoed when water droplets fell (the acoustics were phenomenal and muffled at the same time, odd). Jesus and I had a long conversation. Well, it was more like a stand-off if I'm honest. Jesus wanted me to unlock the cell that held my heart, to let her out to roam free.

But the cell wasn't so much a prison as it was protection for me, or at least I thought so when I put my emotions down there. The idea of letting my heart out to be wounded some more was petrifying. I didn't trust the world, myself, or Jesus to protect her or value her in any way. I was so afraid of this invitation that I couldn't move. I couldn't unlock the door. During this prayer vision it became clear that I wasn't ready to be cracked open in that way. This fierce grace God offered me was too scary. So Jesus, being the stud that he is, told me that he would wait with me in the dungeon as long as it took for me to be ready to let my heart out of the cell. I didn't believe him (have I mentioned that I have deep trust issues?) and had turned to walk out of the dungeon. But I turned back to look at him and he was sitting on the ground, next to my heart's cell door. In front of him was a board game (maybe Monopoly?), and he looked up and smiled at me. He said, "We can stay here as long as it takes." Remembering this still makes me teary at the patience and fierce grace God extends to me.

Mindy and I ended the direction session by agreeing that we would hold my resistance in prayer. I promised that I would spend more time with Jesus in prayer in the dungeon in an attempt to loosen and release my fear. It took a while for me to be willing to open that cell door. Two weeks if I remember correctly. Two weeks is a long time in my interior world. I tend to fly through my internal resistance in a day or two, and if something sticks with me for longer than a week I know that something drastic is amiss. Because of my stubborn perseverance and desire to move forward, I kept returning to this prayer vision. I pondered it, I talked with Jesus about it, I tried to come at this deep-seated fear in different ways to make it come unstuck. It took two weeks of me intentionally and repeatedly returning to the prayer vision to muster up the courage to consider opening up my heart's cell door. When I did gain the courage and returned to the prayer vision to open the door, my little heart was in the cell in suspended animation, floating in mid-air. I held her in my hands and offered her to Jesus (FYI- this was a terrifying act of surrender for me). He smiled at me and in such a gentle way said, "Thank you for wanting me to have your heart, but you need her more than I do. You keep her and take care of her. She will be safe with you." So I kept her. At this point in the prayer vision, my heart actually went into my body where the heart is supposed to be. I was still terrified, still distrustful, especially of myself, but I was slightly more integrated after those couple weeks of deep internal wrestling with fierce grace.

It was in those two weeks of internal grappling that fierce grace worked in me in ways I couldn't begin to appreciate at the time. What I realize now is that Jesus' presence with me, his patience, his deep and abiding compassion, his holding of sacred space was fierce grace in action through one of the members of the Trinity. I had hidden away so much pain that it was eating me from the inside out. I was so distrustful of my emotions that I pretended they didn't exist. However, fierce grace was offering me a more compelling option of how to relate to my heart. This prayer vision helped open something in me so that I could take a small step in being able to honor my emotions in a healthy and beneficial way. I didn't find a rotten, maggot-infested walnut when I cracked myself open. I actually found beauty and love as I looked at myself through the eyes of Jesus, even if I was unwilling to admit it at the time.

The Beating

The journey of honoring my pain and listening to my heart continued into 2013 when I was going through the Spiritual Exercises of Ignatius of Loyola (known as "the Exercises"). Ignatius is known for encouraging people to use imaginative prayer when reading scripture in order to enter into a more intimate relationship with God. His method of making the scriptures come to life is based on using our imaginations to prayerfully experience a scripture passage, noticing what we smell, taste, touch, hear, see, and feel in the setting. I was doing the Exercises in daily life, and I was both transfixed and quite taken aback by the interior movements of my soul in response to God's fierce grace that showed up on many occasions.

During one of the prayer times I was using the scripture where it describes Jesus being beaten and whipped by the Roman guards. I was imagining the scene, noticing what senses were engaged and how I was feeling as I took it all in. My imagination led me to see Jesus chained to a post as he was whipped by the guards. Jesus had been disrobed and was covered with sweat, blood, and dust. The "SNAP" of the whip on his flesh was piercing and tortuous for me. I was standing there in the crowd watching this unfold, watching my beloved be punished because of Love, and I couldn't take it anymore. I rushed in front of the guards screaming, ready to take a gash or a beating for Christ. Very quickly two other guards picked me up by my arms and carried me away. I was kicking and screaming in the imaginative prayer time, trying to get away so that I could get back to Jesus. Unfortunately I was just as small in my imaginative prayer as I am in real life, so I had no chance of getting away from the gigantic guards. My feet never touched the ground as they carried me off.

I talked with Mindy about this particular prayer time, and she asked me questions about what I was feeling during that prayer experience. What I remember telling her was that it felt like my emotions were too big, that I couldn't handle them, that I might crumble if I actually felt them, and that I wouldn't be able to be put back together. I was still very afraid for my heart.

Four plus years after completing the Exercises, I again spoke with Mindy about God and my emotions. During our conversation, I realized that I had become comfortable enough with my emotions to not be scared of them breaking me. I had carried the image of a crumbled pile of rubble as descriptive of what would happen to me if I let myself experience the full emotional weight of my feelings. In this direction session in November 2017, I realized that this image of rubble had become untrue. I realized that I was stronger than I had given myself credit for. This was a really big deal, and I felt like I could finally honor my emotions and heart in a way that brought life and love to me, while not being completely consumed by them. Then Shaq died two months later, and I've been learning what it means to fully experience my emotions while letting myself be transformed by fierce grace through love and loss.

Honoring the Brokenness

I've come to appreciate that honoring grief, pain, and loss requires a fair amount of courage and a willingness to be broken open to be healed and set free by fierce grace, or at least be willing to grow from the brokenness. When Shaq died in late-January 2018, I was broken open completely against my will. I wanted more years with my fuzzy beast, and I wasn't ready to let her go. But that choice was made for me regardless of what I wanted. Yet twenty-four hours after her death, I was sitting in our spot on the floor crying and praying (they were the same at that point, let's be real), allowing myself to feel the full extent of my grief and pain. Tears streamed down my face, and I had created a pile of tissues by my side that had the potential to physically overtake me at any moment.

As I sat there weeping, I had the surprising desire to learn from this terribly painful event. Thanks to fierce grace, a spontaneous prayer for both me and my husband rose up from my depths. "I want us to have more compassion, kindness, and generosity because of this experience." This prayer got my attention. Who prays this kind of prayer when they're in the abyss of grief? Seriously? Where did this come from? Well I knew that it had come from God, and I was taken aback. This prayer of fierce grace became the drum beat keeping time for me over the next few months. I kept returning to this spontaneous and surprising prayer. I let it inform my actions, attitudes, and speech towards others. I hope that I (and my husband) continue to increase in compassion, kindness, and generosity.

When I think about it, this is one of my prayers for myself and the world. I want everyone to grow in compassion, kindness, and generosity through experiencing fierce grace, which will probably happen in times of pain and grief. I hope that I'm growing in the ability to show myself grace, to allow myself to have feelings and not suppress them, to honor my emotions and not get stuck in the grief itself. On a universal level I think we all deeply desire healing and wholeness, *shalom*, for ourselves and the world, even if we're not consciously aware of this desire. However, healing and wholeness require a break-down of the internal walls (a.k.a. shells) that keep us separated and skeptical (even distrusting) of God, others, and ourselves. Yet being open to fierce grace's work in times of suffering can transform us by increasing our kindness, generosity, and compassion.

There's no way around it, grief leaves a scar on our hearts. If we hold our pain with honor and dignity, we can experience fierce grace in the midst of our suffering as I continued to do with the loss of Shaquille.

Chapter 4

Cleaning House & Hanging On

Within twenty-four hours of her death, I suspected that there were a lot of layers tied up in my grief, but I knew I'd need time and space to unpack what might be present. Instead of being present to my feelings, I came home and proceeded to clean most of the house after I returned from saying goodbye to Shaquille at the animal hospital. I started with the living room, Shaq's domain. I vacuumed, pulled up the two carpets, put her house in a trash bag, put her hay, bedding and food in another bag, and intermittently sobbed through the process. I decided that staring at the empty space where she had lived was too much, and I rearranged the living room furniture so I couldn't sit on the couch and look at where she used to sit.

One of my good friends owned one of Shaq's brothers from another litter. That pet also had a larger-than-life personality and had to be put to sleep because of an injury. I remember my friend telling me that before her son and husband came home from the vet that last time, she pulled all of their sweet bunny's things out of the house and hid them. They also didn't want the visual reminder of what they had lost. The painful reminders in the stuff can seem like too great a burden to bear.

And at the same time, both my friend and I have held on to things that can't be used again. Unbeknownst to me, I had done the same thing with Shaq's house as she did with her bunny's house: we put them in trash bags and then hid them in the basement. If either one of us ever get another pet, we know that the houses can't be reused. There's no logical reason for keeping them, especially hidden in the basement. But we can't get rid of them. There's a strong emotional attachment to this place where our beloveds lived. Stuff brings a sense of comfort and normalcy when loved ones are lost. This is a perfectly normal reaction to the loss of a pet. Healing from grief comes in all different shapes, sizes, and speeds. There is no linear path to healing, and getting another pet wasn't going to fill the hole left from death.

Unfortunately, grief isn't rational (as much as I wish it were otherwise!). It ebbs and flows, waxes and wanes, takes us by surprise, and even when we try to forget it, grief refuses to go away without being acknowledged. I was running in my favorite spot a couple months after Shaquille passed and noticed I was super crabby and annoyed with all the people on the trail, especially people and their unleashed dogs. Two days later I was out at the same spot again and noticed again that I was really grumpy. There weren't any people to be mad at this time. I was alone with the cold wind stinging my face, alone with my thoughts, alone with the crunching of my feet against the stone pathway. So, I asked myself as I ran, "Hey body and heart, what is happening?" After some silence and waiting, I remembered what day it was. It was the twenty-seventh. It was exactly two months since Shaq died. I put my hands over my heart and let out a sob. My heart demanded that this day be acknowledged. It was something I hadn't experienced before. I hadn't lost anything or anyone that was such an integral part of my life, and this grief continually takes me by surprise. Grief isn't rational, but its expression is desperately needed.

At fierce grace's prodding, I gave myself the space to be quiet, taciturn even on the twenty-seventh of the month throughout 2018. By giving myself this emotional breathing room, I allowed myself to be with the feelings that rose up from within, even if I was working or in a meeting. With this conscious choice I gave my body and heart the permission to feel whatever they wanted, to be free to be tense or tired or antsy or whatever they needed to be. It was amazing to see how this permission-giving shifted my sense of that day of the month and my awareness of myself. I didn't feel like I was ready to burst at the seams or was angry with everyone around me. I could be sad and that was okay. There was a very distinct freedom in allowing myself to feel and not making apologies for it. Even many months later, I am still taken aback by my grief. My grief feels most strong when the twenty-seventh falls on a Saturday, mimicking the date and day of the week on which Shaq died.

Giving ourselves space to grieve is often so difficult. In my younger days I had a tendency to immerse myself in work in such a dramatic way that I wouldn't have to admit that I had feelings. It was all about doing the right thing, living into an over-developed sense of duty and obligation that was unhealthy. We can throw ourselves into volunteer work, paid work, travel, fishing, redecorating, dating, or baking to try to take our minds off of the one thing that we so deeply miss or don't want to face. I kept myself very busy in my twenties and early thirties because I wasn't willing to deal with the pain, disappointment, fear, and loss buried deep in my soul.

As I know from experience, running from and ignoring pain only causes more pain and grief. I have a long and well-established history of running from my emotions. I'm reminded of a Sunday school class in the summer between my eighth and ninth-grade years. I was going out with someone from church and wasn't into him anymore. So, I wrote him a note to break up with him. Somehow my mom (who was the Sunday school teacher) noticed the note and went to take it. I must have turned a rainbow of colors as I grabbed the note and ran to the bathroom because my mom followed me to the bathroom and kept asking if I was okay. All I wanted was to be left alone and hide in the shame of my emotions being on display in what I thought was such a transparent way. I was absolutely mortified. Granted it was junior high and everything is total drama at that age, but my reaction was fairly over the top even for junior high. I couldn't fathom owning my feelings, and this pattern of running from and hiding my emotions continued well into adulthood.

Unacknowledged Grief

During a conversation with Mindy (it was within the first year of us meeting for spiritual direction), she asked me if I knew how to grieve. I think I looked at her like she had three heads, probably said something very defensive and stupid, and then said, "No, I have no idea." We talked about what might happen if I gave myself the space to grieve. She mentioned that it was quite possible that at some point I would start to cry and have zero mental awareness for why it was happening. She mentioned that it was completely acceptable, welcome even, to have no idea what I might be crying over, and in the tears the grief would be released. Mindy said that sometimes it was better not to know what the grief was, since that wasn't the important part of this process. The important part was the physical, emotional, and spiritual release that the tears signified; the letting go, the relief, the relinquishment of clutching tightly or stuffing my emotions down the well. I wasn't enthused. I didn't cry…or that's what I told myself.

Unacknowledged grief is a very heavy burden to carry. I think of the image from Dickens' *A Christmas Carol* (the movie version with George C. Scott as Scrooge, of course!) where Marley visits Scrooge and is carrying the chains he created in his life. Granted, Marley had his chains for a different reason; selfishness, greed, and a general lack of charity and good will towards all people. However, I think the emotional result is the same with grief, pain, and loss. If we don't work through our grief and let it flow in healthy ways, we end up building a chain, link by link, that slowly but surely becomes an unbearable weight around our necks. Eventually we succumb to the weight of the chain. If the weight is not released, I believe we end up dying a slow emotional death, whether it's becoming mean, overcompensating in some aspect of our lives, focusing on others while ignoring self-care, or however it may show up in us. Because of my life choices, I had created a very heavy chain and had started to stumble from its weight.

I went about life with Mindy's words haunting my thoughts, and less than twelve months later it happened. I had direction with Mindy at her church office and then headed to seminary for class. As I walked to my car the tears started to flow for no conscious reason. I sobbed as I drove the half hour to school. I was already running late, and I tried to pull myself together to go in for class. Nope, that wasn't happening. My grief had been uncorked like a bottle of sparkling wine, and the pressure refused to be contained. I sat in my car in the seminary parking lot for at least thirty minutes with tears flowing down my face like a waterfall. And I had no idea why I was crying. None, whatsoever. I had been carrying around so much emotional stuff that when it finally came out, I felt like I had been run over by a truck. I was emotionally, mentally, and physically exhausted, almost numb from the purging of the stored emotional burden. As I look back on this experience, I think fierce grace cheered (in a kind and loving way). "It's starting!" She cried with glee. "Out with the old ways and in with the new! She's starting to be open to this kind of transformation." As I believe fierce grace knew so well that day, this purging was a breakthrough. It marked a turning point in my journey. From that moment forward I knew that my pattern of ignoring my feelings had become very unhealthy. I could not ignore the bad habits that needed to change, and fierce grace was there to help me.

If we're bold and courageous enough, eventually we will sit with the pain and allow fierce grace to do her work. We will live in the tension between holding on to things and wanting to purge. We will acknowledge the grief, hold it, and welcome it with open arms. We will examine grief's facets to see what we can glean from the experience. I can't bury my feelings anymore, no matter how hard I try. And for me this has been one of my best lessons learned from fierce grace: I don't need to apologize for my tears. They are mine. I own them. If they make someone else uncomfortable, that's their problem.

Job, Misfortune, and Friends

During the several months after Shaquille passed, grief became a friend, a reminder that I was still, in fact, alive. When we lose someone or something, we must accept that for a time, pain and grief will be our constant companions. And yet as time goes on, we also can notice how these companions shift, change, swell, and recede. We can honor our emotions by naming them and allowing them to be present without trying to force them away.

I love the story of Job in the Old Testament. If there's anybody whose life went down the crapper in a hurry, it was his. The "accuser" (*ha-satan* in Hebrew) convinced God to let him destroy Job's family, business, and health. God and the accuser basically bet on whether Job will curse God because of the misfortune that will befall him. God thinks Job will persevere and the accuser thinks Job will give in. Job was somewhat distraught at first, but he didn't curse God and die like his wife suggested. Instead he sat outside the gate to his town and picked at his sores with pieces of broken pottery. Good times. When Job's friends heard about his misfortune, they came to sit with him outside of the gate to the city, to be present in his suffering. For the first week, words were not spoken, as if there was this silent acknowledgement that the situation was too big, too encompassing for words.

But after seven days, Job's friends started speaking. They told him that Job must have done something wrong, that he was unrighteous in some way, and that he needed to admit it. Only after admitting that he had done something wrong would God restore his life to him. Job didn't buy it. He argued with his friends that he had done nothing wrong, that he had lived a blameless life, and also that he had made sacrifices for himself and his children in case they accidentally sinned and didn't realize it. The more his friends tried to convince him to confess and repent, the more frustrated Job became. He started to rail against God, saying that he wanted a hearing so that he could defend himself against this undeserved misfortune that had befallen him. Job came across as arrogant and delusional to his friends, and they kept arguing about Job's state of righteousness.

When God showed up to Job at the end of the story, God told Job that he was right. Job was righteous, yet he suffered all the same. Granted, we wouldn't have the story of Job if his friends had stayed silent. But sometimes presence is more important than speech. If Job's friends would have been a bit wiser, they might have been able to notice and act on this understanding. I have several takeaways from the book of Job, one of which is to not be as reductive as Job's friends. Suffering has nothing to do with righteousness or a lack thereof.

Fierce grace has shown me that having a strong, wise, and loving group of friends and/or family to support and walk with us in these first few months after loss is vital. Like my friends and family rearranged their schedules for me when Shaq died, my husband and I did the same thing when my step-father-in-law got sick. My husband and I generally stay to ourselves and don't visit family as much as we should, but when my step-father-in-law was diagnosed with terminal pancreatic cancer, we visited my mother-in-law and step-father-in-law every few weeks. Fierce grace was telling me that regardless of whether we thought we had the time, we needed to make time because Ethan was not going to live very long. We needed to show up physically to be a support for Ethan and Leigh during the preparation for his death. We understood that our presence was incredibly important. After Ethan's passing, we continued visiting more consistently to check in on Leigh and make sure she was as okay as could be expected. Leigh's sisters and brothers also made their presence known in new or different ways. Although we encouraged her to eat something other than cheese, crackers, and beer, we were unsuccessful. This wasn't the first time she lived on that diet and won't be the last. [As an aside: My brother-in-law got Leigh cheese and crackers for Christmas this year and she remarked, "This is great! I have dinner for three weeks." She loves her cheese and crackers.] We stayed with Leigh, and we were present as witnesses to her grief and our collective grief. And after about a year and a half, Leigh started to live life again, which was not only a beautiful thing to see but also a huge relief to her family.

So Many Layers

I have several friends who supported me through the loss of my precious (and precocious) bunny, and I also have a spiritual director who is doggedly relentless in helping me see God's invitations of fierce grace in the midst of whatever turmoil I happen to be in when we talk. Thanks to Mindy and our direction sessions, I noticed fairly immediately after Shaq died that through the loss of our bunny, fierce grace was uncovering deeper issues that God wanted me to confront and allow God to heal. Fierce grace was working through my suffering in a way I had not experienced before.

I have a distinct sense of right and wrong and am willing to put my personal needs aside for the good of the order or common good, whatever that might be. With Shaq's health, my husband and I did everything right. We increased her hay consumption, we reduced the amount of pellets she got, we stopped feeding her papaya bites, and we gave her organic kale (holy cow did she love kale!). We fed her on a schedule, made sure she got exercise, had snuggle time, and took her to the vet for checkups.

And yet none of this stopped her fussy digestive system from revolting. We did everything right and it didn't matter. That voice, the inner critic, ego, or whatever you want to call it that says "If you do the right thing, everything will work out the way it should (according to me)" is a liar, because Shaq died even though we did everything right. That deep-seated narrative of my life was dealt a death blow after years of being picked at and poked and prodded by fierce grace.

Doing things the right way meant that I had control over my life, and I liked that control. For most of my life I have been guided by a spirit of self-reliance. You might think self-reliance is a good thing; we need to be independent, self-sufficient, and capable people for a functioning society. Yes, these things might be good for us to a certain extent, but my self-reliance used to be and still can be pathological. The inner monologue includes things like the following: "No one can help me, not even God." "If others help me, then I didn't do a good enough job." "If things are to be done right, then I have to do them myself." "I can't accept help from others, it will make me a bad or weak person." Do you see the dysfunction? The illusion of control permeates my false narratives.

When my "rightness and control" narrative broke, I felt like the oxygen was sucked out of the room. In early February I had another direction session with Mindy. As we talked I told her about how I felt like my Enneagram Type One need for control and rightness got run over. Smushed. Cracked. Broken. The "rightness" compulsion in me broke, like a child's toy that was stepped on and broken to pieces. Mindy remarked that this was such a beautiful invitation to let go of the need to be right and enforce rightness. It may have been true, but it felt more like an external force imposing this on me as opposed to me being able to choose my response to it. What I noticed during this conversation was that I had no desire to put the pieces back together. Rightness had been ripped out of me and then stomped on with me watching. It was like fierce grace was taunting me, "Oh, you thought you did the right thing? Well let's see about that. This is what I think of your rightness." Stomp. Crush. Crunch. A significant part of me, my desire to uphold rightness, which was something that I intensely protected and cherished, died that day. And in reality I needed to let it go.

I needed to let it go because rightness was a protection mechanism. If I do the right thing, then nothing bad should happen. If I take the high road, I did the right thing and can feel good about myself even if the situation didn't turn out well. If I work my tail off, no one can say I did the wrong thing or didn't put in enough effort. Rightness theoretically ensured I wouldn't be criticized, I wouldn't be wrong, I couldn't be hurt. (Type Ones are notoriously hard on themselves, wickedly so, if they're unhealthy, and external criticism just makes the inner critic worse.) All of this striving was motivated by a deep desire for protection from failure and criticism. The false narrative needed to die along with Shaquille. And it's still dying a slow and painful death because it has been a part of me for ten times longer than Shaq was with us. Giving up the illusion of control has been a very hard pill for me to swallow, because being in control and being right gives me a feeling of self-righteousness, that I'm better than others around me and this can get me into trouble.

I remember when one of my first spiritual mentors told Daisy (my prayer partner) and me that you can go from having a spiritual PhD to being back in kindergarten in a hot minute. At the time both of us were like, "Yeah, yeah, that won't happen to us." But it did, over and over again. It is incredibly humbling to think you're finally getting your spiritual life together only to be reoriented to see yourself in a way that is humiliating and shameful (or at least that's how I internalized these revelations at the time). Pride definitely comes before a fall. For me, it's usually my tongue that gets me into unfortunate situations for which I need to apologize. I was at a random Wednesday morning Bible study during seminary and the topic of communion during Easter services came up. I made some snide comment about how the senior pastor and I disagree on whether communion should be served at all three worship services (it wasn't and still isn't for various logistical reasons). The ladies' faces displayed visible shock that I was publicly expressing my displeasure with our pastor's choice, and I realized that I had made a big mistake. I ended up calling the pastor later that day and apologizing for running my mouth since it was his church to lead and not mine. He accepted my apology very gracefully, and my bad decision didn't put a dent in our relationship. But even seven or eight years later, I'm still somewhat embarrassed by this incident. I was brought from PhD discourse to playground gossip in the blink of an eye.

One of many things I've learned from life is that fierce grace isn't concerned with keeping my pride intact. This type of episode happened more than I care to admit as I was finding my way in the early years of my spiritual awakening. Emotions, false beliefs, and bad behaviors were being purged, usually at a significant cost to my pride. Because of this reorientation, I had to reevaluate what I thought was acceptable behavior and what wasn't. It took me ten years to realize that being kind is more important than being right, although I still sometimes choose being right over being kind if I'm tired, hungry, or stressed.

As much as this return to spiritual kindergarten was incredibly painful when it first began happening, I've noticed that as I've matured in my faith, I don't see the return in the same way anymore. The idea of returning to kindergarten isn't filled with shame nor is it humiliating, which is huge growth for me. I'm now more fascinated than anything else, because I'm reminded that every one of my deep-seated behaviors and thought patterns has layers—lots and lots of layers. Every time a layer is peeled back and fierce grace reveals something new to reconcile, get rid of, or let go of, Jesus helps me heal again—over and over, layer by layer. Things that I thought were dealt with or worked through have come back up in direction with Mindy more times than I can count. Most recently I've noticed that I haven't been frustrated with this pattern. Instead I've been joyful that God is revealing some new way to increase my *shalom*.

In my last direction session of 2018, Mindy and I got to explore a new layer of personal dysfunction where I believed that the Christian journey must be difficult and require hard work because I thought Jesus' ministry was unpleasant, painful, and tedious. She asked me what the hard work gave me, and without a second thought I said "self-righteousness." There it was again. I was fascinated that my subconscious was harboring this false belief while simultaneously bolstering my ego. I was slightly embarrassed to say that self-righteousness was the prize in all of my slogging for Jesus, but at the same time, it was a huge relief to name it. Once it was named and unpacked in my direction session it lost a lot of its power, and I became freer and more whole.

Fierce grace knows I need to be reminded every day that life is a journey and not a destination. My spiritual journey is a layer by layer walk that seems to repeatedly circle back through the same themes like a downward spiral. The deeper I go, the more layers fierce grace peels off, the more healed and whole I become. I now look forward to these revelations since experience has taught me that peeling back the layers offers inexplicable freedom that I couldn't create for myself.

Realistically, I'm not sure there's enough time on earth to explore all the layers of my control issues and pathological self-reliance. The control freak in me pops up and takes over when I'm tired, too busy, or ignoring my body's messages for self-care. I don't want to inflict my version of crazy onto other people, but I do it anyway without realizing it most of the time. Acknowledging this thought and behavior pattern is its own kind of surrender to spiritual kindergarten, as embarrassing as it might be. Fierce grace repeatedly reminds me that I don't actually have control of control. As much as I would like to delete the last several paragraphs because I want people to think I have it all together, that I do the right thing all the time, and that my life is under control, it's not, and it most likely never will be.

I want people to think of me as someone who has a clean house, both internally and externally. But that isn't the reality, is it? My internal and external houses are a mess, as much as I would like to admit otherwise. Yes, I can clean toilets when I'm upset, rearrange the furniture when I experience loss, or reduce clutter when I have "too much" emotional energy or feel tied down. In some ways, these are healthy options for dealing with grief and loss. But eventually the house is clean, the closets are clear, and the toilet can wait a day before being scrubbed again. If we listen to fierce grace's invitation to be present with our grief (even amid ferocious cleaning), she will reveal the next layer in God's timing. Sometimes the next layer has to do with healing our emotions. Other times it has to do with reworking our identities, chunk by chunk, until we're able to see ourselves as God sees us.

Chapter 5

Losing My Identity

I had a conversation with a clergy colleague the other day about mid-life crises. He was thinking that he needed to schedule his mid-life crisis, like someone can actually decide when they're going to have a life-altering meltdown. We talked about his understanding of a mid-life crisis: one in which he would take stock of his career, personal possessions and finances, life choices, relationship status, etc. After doing a mental tabulation of these things, he would then compare himself to where he thought he would be at this time in life and then compare himself to others and where they're at. As you can probably imagine, I pushed back on this idea. I shared that as a Christian, having a traditional mid-life crisis probably wasn't the best choice (especially if you're planning it out) because it focused on material wealth, possessions, and cultural comparisons. As Christians, we're not supposed to be holding up a measuring stick to our material lives and comparing it with other people. Theoretically, our bank accounts, education, or job descriptions don't give us value as human beings. Being created in God's image gives us our inherent value and identity.

What if there was a better option to the traditional mid-life crisis? What if a mid-life crisis could be a reordering of values and conscience, what is most important in our lives? What if, like Richard Rohr describes in his book *Falling Upward*, we go from being focused on success, wealth, and gaining stability to evaluating what we believe, why we believe it, and what we truly want out of life so we can pursue the things that actually matter instead of chasing the desperate dreams of wealth and excessive consumerism forced on us from an early age? I don't think my colleague fully received what I was suggesting.

This conversation with him made me think about how we identify ourselves. What is the leading descriptor that we use when asked about ourselves? Is it our job? Our role in the family? An organizational membership? Our sexual orientation? Race or religion? How we see ourselves factors heavily into who we are as people, where our treasure lies, and how we prioritize our time, talents, and gifts. We sometimes are under the mistaken impression that what we do, what we produce, or what group we belong to is a main factor in our identities.

Vocational Identity

In September 2009 I was laid off from my engineering job. I was stunned to find out because in my mind I was safe. At the time I was laid off, I was ninety-five percent billable, which means that I charged clients a preset hourly rate (let's say $75/hour) for ninety-five percent of my time on the job. To me, this meant that I was making good money for the company and that my job was secure. Nope, apparently not—at least, not with the second part of that sentence. I didn't realize that my job could be easily split up and given to higher-level and lower-level employees. I had developed relationships with our clients, and I liked helping design solutions from the ground up. I enjoyed the creativity of exploring potential solutions and designing spaces, treatment systems, and layouts for equipment. Even though I was in seminary and knew God had something else waiting for me, I was heavily invested in my identity as an engineer. I loved the creative work of it and felt it was the most significant part of who I was.

Because I was laid off, it gave me time to consider what my options were and what I might do to bring additional income to our household. It also gave me time to use my engineering and project management skills as the volunteer project coordinator for the Habitat Women Build (through which I also learned some excellent community development and fundraising skills). I was torn between finding another engineering job and diving into ministry in some way. Being in seminary meant my schedule would change every semester, which wasn't a good look for potential employers. Even if my credentials were better than another, I couldn't promise that I'd be in the office from eight a.m. to five p.m. every day. I had other obligations and couldn't, in good conscience, go out looking for a full-time position without disclosing this information. Apart from the fact that there weren't very many full-time environmental engineering positions available, I was not getting calls about my resume.

Full-time employment also offers the perk of a decent salary. Money doesn't buy happiness, but it does buy choices. Once I was laid off, we had severely limited choices. After a while (about nine months to a year) with no engineering job leads, I realized that maybe I had to give up this significant piece of my identity, which was difficult because I had my parents consistently prodding me to go back to engineering, thinking that I would be wasting my degree if I didn't continue with engineering in some way. Not surprisingly, being an engineer defined who I was for a long time and was more important than the fact that I was a Christian, in Christ.

Over the next few years I had to figure out who I wanted to be, distancing myself little by little from my former vocational identity. This was not an easy task, especially when I was driving back and forth to seminary once or twice per week, was going through a dark night of the soul, had started an anti-depressant and anti-anxiety medication, couldn't get pregnant, and was seriously wrestling with my call to professional ministry. The medication treated the physical symptoms of my identity crisis: the desire to peel my skin off at any given moment, to run screaming out of Target when I couldn't find "Merry Christmas" wrapping paper, and to quit the whole damn institution of church that seemed to hurt people more often than it helped people.

With my layoff as the starting point to my complete identity reworking, every aspect of me as a human being was torn apart and separated by fierce grace so that eventually I could be put back together again in a new way with new and old pieces and parts. Fierce grace was inviting me to see myself as a container that held a narrative that was no longer useful, helpful, or life-giving. It felt like I was being turned inside out, shaken upside down like a backpack or purse to make sure there wasn't anything left in me, to ensure I was void. I didn't appreciate the void. Fierce grace invited me to carry around an empty vessel for a while. With help from Mindy and Bill, over time (lots of time, like several years) I embraced the emptiness and was able to let the old stories go. As I held my empty vessel and waited, I realized that fierce grace might have new stories waiting for me.

The part that I now remember most clearly about this vocational-identity reconstruction during 2009-2010 was the realization (thanks to fierce grace) that my identity, how I choose to see myself, is up to me. For a long time I identified myself as "an engineer," then a "former engineer." I merged the questions "who are you" and "what do you do." But they aren't the same thing. I was under the mistaken belief that I was worthless if I didn't have a job that contributed to society in a "meaningful" way. In God's eyes, value and vocation are in no way tied to each other, yet I didn't understand this concept. "What do you do?" is an ice-breaker question that gives a bit of insight into a person. If I answered, "I am an engineer," people could assume that I was good at math and science and that I had an undergraduate degree. They could ask follow up questions about the kind of work I did and where I got my degree. Being an environmental engineer said something about what I valued and how I wanted to be perceived in the world. My value was tied up in what I was doing, producing, and changing for the better. It was championing for my clients, getting them grant money, and finding solutions to their treatment system problems.

Image and Messaging

Three of my closest friends have a JD (law degree) or PhD. Apparently, I like to hang with a brainy crowd. What I've noticed in observing my friends is that there's a certain way they carry themselves and move in the world as smart, talented, and creative women. They present themselves in a manner that is both unassuming yet powerful, and this is intentional on their parts. What they do and how they present themselves is part of the messaging that they send out into the world.

We all have messages that we transmit, regardless of whether it is conscious or subconscious. There are distinct choices we make that provide a specific narrative of ourselves, how we want to be perceived, our success, status, etc. All these things relate to our desire to control our lives and our lack of surrender to our real identity. My three brainy friends and I have been through a very distinct professional culling process (based on layoffs, job changes, being passed over for promotion, not taken seriously as women, etc.) where we have been forced to confront the difference between how we want to be seen by the world and who we actually are. Our false selves, the images and public personas we created for ourselves to present to the world, needed to be released because they were not an authentic representation of the people whom God created. Our true selves, the authentically and uniquely created persons each one of us has been from conception, wanted to be unleashed so that we could experience life more fully. We had a choice between continuing to boost our false selves at significant emotional peril or letting the false selves go one piece at a time.

Granted, none of us are done with this process. Thanks to fierce grace's continued pursuit, each one of us has chosen in some way to let go of the desire to manage how we want to be seen. We have surrendered control of our narratives to God and are living into who we have been created to be. To give a somewhat superficial, albeit important, example, I have started going out of the house without makeup. For those of you (woman or man) who don't wear makeup, this might seem like a weird thing to you. But I was an independent beauty consultant for over fifteen years, and we were told to NEVER go out of the house without our "face" on. We were our best advertising for the product. This has been a hard lesson for me to unlearn. It was a few weeks ago as I was heading to run errands and had gotten in my car when I realized I didn't have any makeup on at all. No foundation, no mascara, nothing. As I looked at myself in the visor mirror I thought, "Well, it's too late to go back now. Whether or not you have makeup on does not impact your value as a human being." Fierce grace was at it again, inviting me to see myself in a way that didn't depend on my false self's messaging and created image. She was encouraging me to see myself as God sees me, with or without makeup. Fierce grace whispered, "Have you considered that curating an image or persona might actually be a waste of energy?"

Going without "my face" in public has been liberating. Wearing makeup has been one of the most consistent ways I've tried to control the messaging I send to the world. If I have makeup on I feel like I'm more put together than if I don't. This isn't true, but the false narrative is still there and is slowly receding into the background. This issue is one of several ways fierce grace has been working within me. The tension between judgment and grace, control and surrender, false self and true self are being reconciled into unity within my own being because of fierce grace's persistent presence.

Despite this internal struggle between opposing forces, I feel like I'm moving towards becoming a more compassionate and kind human being to myself and creation, less inclined to care about how I'm perceived by others and much less concerned with feeding the insatiable ego of my false self. From wrestling with fierce grace, I have been given the opportunity to reflect on my internal monologue and give myself permission to hold my identity loosely. After several years, I believe fierce grace when she tells me that my job does not define me or give me worth, that these externals are not central pillars to my identity as a person. When I'm open to fierce grace, I realize that sometimes part of the story that I've woven for myself becomes untrue, like the fact that I am no less worthy of a human being if I choose not to wear makeup or am not an engineer anymore.

One of my brainy friends noted that the mythological Phoenix is a beautiful metaphor for our journey in this life. It's no wonder the early Christians used the Phoenix as a subversive symbol for Christ. The Phoenix rises from the ashes of death and is reborn anew against all odds. Not only does Christ rise again, but we can too. Fierce grace provides the nudge to let God refine us by fire. It can be a scary invitation. At the same time, what if this refining is what God wants for us, so that our true selves can shine like the Sun? What if fierce grace is inviting us to be reborn into something much more enchanting and magical?

Even entertaining this question from fierce grace can be terrifying. "What do you mean that I can be something other than what I am, what I've studied to be?" I asked God on numerous occasions. When it came to going to seminary, I heard God say that I wasn't useful in my current state. Now whether or not this was God speaking is up for debate because it sounds a bit harsh. Yet I didn't take it personally. I knew in my bones that doing what God wanted required some additional education so I could do it "right." (Enneagram Type 1 dysfunction was so strong in 2007!)

This transformation into "usefulness" (with or without a master's degree) is what fierce grace invites us to. She is focused whole-heartedly on our transformation because God wants us to live from our authentic natures and true selves. We can't do that if we're holding on to a false persona or listening to our egos all the time. If we notice, listen to, and respond to the nudges from fierce grace, we can be remade into the people God created us to be before we accepted and lived into the identities placed on us by culture, our families, and ourselves.

What if we're being invited to courageously and authentically answer the question, "Who are you?"

Who am I?

"Who are you?" is a deep, rich, beautiful, and theological question. It calls out the best and worst in us, which can be frightening. According to my husband, Pat, I am weird, frustrating, very book smart, funny (by accident most of the time), an advertiser's worst nightmare, a good (but super messy) cook, and stubborn. Because of my deadpan inflection, Pat can never tell when I'm actually throwing shade his way, or if it's just morning and I'm not ready for people quite yet.

If I'm being realistic, some of the quirky things in my personality won't go away because they're part of who I am. They are knit within me in such a way that they are me, giving me my personality, talents, gifts, and abilities. My desire to be better, to do better, to make the world better is part of me (especially as an Enneagram Type One). But with age and incrementally larger amounts of wisdom, I'm learning how to temper and soften this natural inclination. And these quirks may never go away. It has taken me a decade to be comfortable living into these characteristics. But even so, these personality traits aren't who I am at my core. I am a child of God. My value comes from being created in love and light and beauty and grace. My value does not come from my vocation, what I produce, or how I help people. Those are expressions of the fact that I am a child of God and have been created to bless the world in a unique way.

The choice to believe first and foremost that I am a child of God, regardless of how screwed up I might be on a given day is what I choose to embrace. And everyone can answer "I am a child of God" if they want. But it didn't occur to me for some time after being laid off that my vocation did not add value to me as a human being. I am a child of God, a beloved child of God. That is who I am, and it took several years, many spiritual direction sessions, and the Ignatian Spiritual Exercises for me to get there. I still describe myself as a former engineer with a never-ending love for spreadsheets (I even created a spreadsheet to tally how many words I typed for this book each week so I could keep on track. So good!). But the difference now is that I am using these descriptors as personality characteristics and not as a defining set of identifiers. I am a child of God and with that comes the intrinsic reminder that I am enough. By God's grace, I am enough in and through Christ, as difficult as this might be to accept sometimes.

Fierce Grace and the Inner Critic

One of the things that has become most important in my identity journey has been the ability to give myself grace. Grace, technically defined for those of you not familiar with this Christian term, is unmerited favor. Christians use the term grace primarily regarding God's relationship with human beings. God gives us grace. We have unmerited favor in God's eyes. We are included in God's family for no other reason than God loves us and wants to be in relationship with us. There is nothing we can do to earn or deserve God's love. This is the gift of God's grace.

Grace can also be more loosely defined as mercy, space, compassion, or cutting someone some slack. I am an Enneagram Type One, fixated on perfectionism and a relentless pursuit of "better." I judge everything against an incomprehensible and unattainable ideal of what my life should be. There's not a lot of grace naturally included in my inner monologue. It's a big freaking deal to intentionally see myself as enough, to give myself space for making a mistake, for not reaching a goal, or for not being perfect.

I've had to work at this grace-giving very intentionally over several years. One of the things I didn't notice at first about going on an anti-depressant was that my inner critic or ego voice disappeared. It wasn't until I went off the medication that the voice came back with a vengeance. I had started the Ignatian Spiritual Exercises in January 2013, doing imaginative prayer for an hour or more each day as guided by Mindy. At the end of March, I stopped the medication and noticed a huge difference in my thought process and how I saw myself. The voice in my head was meaner, more hateful, and stronger than I remembered. I couldn't do anything right. I got an "A" on my independent study paper that semester, and it wasn't good enough. The voice told me that all the comments on my paper should have been positive comments and no constructive criticism should have been included. Basically, the paper wasn't perfect so I was worth less than gum stuck to the bottom of a shoe. Having this inner critic's monologue run constantly though my head was too much to bear. I couldn't believe how much I hated myself.

Mindy and I talked about it during one of our Spiritual Exercises sessions. We discussed how there are times to immediately refuse the voice, to tell it it's wrong and reframe the sentence to be more positive. This was how I had operated before the anti-depressant. We also talked about welcoming the voice, giving it space to express itself, sitting with the words or feelings being conveyed. And once the feelings or thoughts were expressed, I could say something like "Thank you ego for wanting to keep me safe, but this is not helpful right now. I'm going to take this risk and see how it works out. There is no shame in failure." Holy cow, this was hard to do. After trying this for a few days without a visual or concrete thing to project onto, I went and found one of my stuffed animals from when I was a kid. Fierce grace had the perfect one in mind.

I wasn't looking for the Cabbage Patch Kid or my Pound Puppy. The perfect representation of the inner critic was a monster from the book Where the Wild Things Are. This stuffed animal has horns, is covered in blue fur, and has a black and gray beard, funky claws, and human feet. I ended up calling this voice "Bossy Mind" and the stuffed animal monster was her visual representation. Bossy Mind was such an integral part of my life that she needed a name. Something I could call her to put her in her place, to remind her that rightness, control, and protection weren't the goals of this life. Whenever I noticed that Bossy Mind was having a fit, I would find the fuzzy monster and hug it. Fierce grace encouraged me to hug the stuffed animal, thanking Bossy Mind for her deep concern for my well-being but that we were going to go a different direction and that life was going to be okay. Fierce grace reminded us that God loves us regardless of whether or not we are perfect. We didn't have to expect perfection and could fail. By acknowledging these false narratives in such a concrete way, fierce grace nudged me closer to *shalom*.

I realize this might sound kind of crazy, but I can't tell you how much hugging this stuffed animal helped quiet this energetic inner critic that waged war against me. Bossy Mind the Monster still sits in my office as a reminder of who I've been and what isn't a healthy inner monologue. One day I realized that Bossy Mind had, for the most part, stopped her frantic yelling. She had relaxed and didn't have to be hyper-vigilant anymore. Every once in a while, I still pick up the stuffed animal and give it a squeeze or pat it on its head and thank it for being part of my journey. After all, Bossy Mind is still a part of me.

This dance between personal judgment and grace has created the flexibility and openness in my personality to not be so hard on myself, to not feel like my world is ending in a shame-filled fire ball when I make a mistake. I also notice when I'm getting rigid and falling into old thought and behavior patterns, which indicates that something is going on with my heart or body that needs to be acknowledged. When I hear Bossy Mind get ramped up, I know something is off kilter and I need to take a moment to regroup. She's now a warning signal in my head instead of a constant voice of criticism and vigilance. She and I have both been embraced by fierce grace.

My mid-life or identity crisis started when I was thirty-one and ended when I turned forty. As I reread this last sentence I thought, "Wow. That's almost a decade of yuck." Yes, yes it was. And it was brilliant. What I have to admit is that I wouldn't be the person I am at forty without those nine years of reworking, imagining, and letting go of who I thought I was supposed to be. I am grateful for fierce grace's work in my life. I'm grateful for these years of searching, striving, letting go, loss, grief, and reordering of everything I thought was important. But I won't sugar coat it: there were parts that have really sucked and there will be terrible parts in the future because that's life. Yet it's been worth the arduous and difficult and grace-filled journey, and it continues to be worth it. I realize I'm only forty and not at all finished with spiritual transformation. But I am content, happy or satisfied maybe, with who I've become by this point in life.

Even though I'm content for now...hmmm, this sounds inaccurate. Maybe content should be in quotes, because I'm not sure anyone would ever describe me as content to be still or stationary for longer than five minutes (unless I'm napping)! So even though I'm "content," I still want to become more Christ-like, more loving, caring, transformative, and compassionate. I want to get better at spiritual direction, coaching, training, and communicating. I want to impact the world in big and small ways. My desire to make the world a better place hasn't gone away because I left environmental engineering. It's just switched from one focus to another (and has become much less compulsive because of fierce grace).

In all of this, I have had to open myself up to fierce grace in the painful and discombobulating journey of letting go; letting go of the false narratives, mistaken identity, and attachment to production and perfectionism. I've had to be willing to receive the Divine's gift of fierce grace, which has transformed me in so many ways, especially in how I see myself and from where I choose my value as a child of God. However, letting go of my former vocation was only one of the ways fierce grace was helping me reorient my identity. There were other identity pieces she wanted to reorder and have me notice, which included how I understand my purpose as a woman.

Chapter 6

What Is Enough?

I used to think forty was old. Now that I've gone through the "decade of yuck," it's been interesting to reflect on how I've changed as a human being thanks to fierce grace's help. Even though I didn't identify her as "fierce grace" before 2018, I can see very strongly how she's been both patient and persistent in prompting me towards seeing myself as enough during the past ten years, especially when it comes to how I live as a female and whether I have biological children.

Pat and I got married in 2003, and I had enough plans and expectations for the both of us. We needed to have steady jobs, buy a house that preferably had four bedrooms and a two-car garage with a nice yard, and then within five years start a family and have two children. In the fall of 2004, we bought our four-bedroom, two-car garage house on 0.39 acres in a little borough that was close enough to work but far enough away from the traffic and hoopla of the nearby college town.

This house was something. To put the décor of the home in perspective for you, the living room had a wallpaper mural of a sunset on one of the walls, and tan, fake wood paneling below the chair rail (this is central PA people. Seriously?). I think the paneling was supposed to mimic sand. The main bathroom was cornflower blue. The walls, the sink, the toilet and the fiberglass tub and surround were all cornflower blue. One would have thought that the house was built in the sixties.

Nope, circa 1985. It was surprisingly tacky, which was why we got a good price for the house. At the time, I worked for a remodeling store, so I was happy to come in and paint all the living areas over a couple years, tear out the carpet and put in laminate flooring, and remove or paint the awful fake wood paneling that was in strategically poor locations. But these were projects that had a visual impact. It turns out that neither Pat nor I like maintaining things. And a house and yard require a large amount of maintenance.

In late 2007 while I was deciding whether to follow God's promptings and go back to school, we (maybe more like I) decided it was time to start a family. This is when things really started to go sideways. Let's just say that once I came off birth control, my body had a hard time finding its rhythm. My cycle was sporadic, ranging from three weeks to six weeks, heavy to light, and I was never sure in those moments past twenty-eight days if I was pregnant or if my cycle was going to be long again. Over the course of the next year or two, I underwent tests to figure out what might be wrong. The doctors found nothing out of the ordinary except for a preliminary diagnosis of polycystic ovarian syndrome (PCOS). The PCOS somewhat explained the lack of rhythm in my menstrual cycle but didn't explain the inability to get pregnant. Things were tried, such as medication to get my body into a twenty-eight day cycle and force ovulation. But after three months of that I had had enough of the trips to the doctor's office. When it got to the point where my doctor said the only other diagnostic option was laparoscopic surgery, Pat put the kibosh on that quickly. My parents offered to pay for additional tests and in-vitro, but that wasn't what Pat and I wanted to do. Nor did we feel comfortable adopting. So I decided to focus on school (by this point I was in my fourth semester at seminary and had been laid off from my engineering job) and let things happen as they may. My desire for children was buried, not left behind.

Then in 2015, the year of suck, Pat and I decided to sell our home, move into an apartment, and give ourselves the space and time to figure out what we really wanted in life. We were both traveling a ton for work and pleasure, and we didn't have the time, money, or energy for weekly yard maintenance and home repairs, at least not on that house. So we cleaned house, literally. We got rid of all kinds of crap that accumulates in eleven years, finished minor projects that had been languishing, and put the house on the market at the beginning of August.

I had found an apartment that was almost all-inclusive of utilities, had free parking, and was centrally located. Unfortunately, alleged drug dealers, each weighing a good 250 pounds, moved in above us. As we were getting settled in our apartment, I woke up one morning with joint pain and stiffness. The stiffness was so bad that I could barely move my hands. This was very odd. But I let it go for a couple days thinking that it was because we had been doing a lot of moving of boxes and furniture, and I was just sore from that. The stiffness persisted. I was paranoid that I was getting rheumatoid arthritis like my grandma, so I went to the doctor. Dr. Rocket told me that he thought it was the move, and it would go away. He saw the skepticism on my face and asked, "Karen, would it make you feel better if you got tested for West Nile, Lyme disease, and rheumatoid arthritis?" I said yes. He was correct; the tests came back negative. Like I said, this was odd, but I let it go and continued the whirlwind schedule that I had, working three different jobs and traveling to the other side of the world.

Luckily for us, we received a good offer on the house within a week of listing. We closed on the sale the same day I left for Mongolia. September 18, 2015 will always be in my memory: six weeks after we put the house up for sale. Pat called me to confirm the house was no longer ours while my colleague and I were waiting for our flight at the airport. Yet the relief wasn't what I thought it would be. After returning from a fifteen-day work trip to Mongolia (the people are lovely and the countryside reminded me of eastern Wyoming), I got a case of vertigo. However, Dr. Rocket said I could travel, so I stocked up on motion-sickness tablets and headed to Thailand for a week at the end of October (the people are also lovely). I didn't realize it at the time, but I was ill for the entire trip. I felt terrible and was unwilling to admit it. I got home, resumed life, and then had a panic attack a week later. All of this added to the stress of the random joint stiffness I continued to have and led to regular arguments with Pat because he couldn't sleep with the noise coming from the apartment upstairs.

Over the 2015 Christmas holiday, my family found out that my brother and his wife were expecting their second child. I was extremely happy for them, knowing that my nephew Michael would do better with a sibling with whom he could fight and share. But after a couple days, I got really depressed. I ended up crying in the guest bedroom at my parents' house, not having any idea why. My mom felt terrible for me and wanted to fix things but knew that she couldn't. I returned home and wondered what was up.

A week later, at the beginning of January 2016, I was on personal retreat and had a direction session with Mindy during my retreat time. As we were on the phone talking, she helped me realize that much of what I was experiencing was rooted in holding on to past expectations and hopes of filling our old house with children. My body was revolting, trying to get my attention to work through this significant loss. I had processed my feelings regarding the status of what it means to own a house and the rejection of that particular American dream. In fact, I was relatively free enough by the time we sold the property that I blessed the house for the next owners and prayed for their happiness and joy to be fulfilled by having a safe place to live.

However, I was completely unaware of the symbolism and spiritual ties between the house and having a family. Fierce grace was trying to get my attention through my body, and I was not getting the message. It had been twelve years since Pat and I got married and five-plus years since we stopped trying to figure out why we couldn't reproduce. It never occurred to me that I was still holding out hope for a biological family. Selling the house was the proverbial nail in the coffin for that dream, and I was not acknowledging this loss. Mindy and I (with God's presence and fierce grace prodding me along) processed these emotions, and I was able to let my dreams of having children go. With Mindy's encouragement, I had a conversation with Jesus about it. It turned out that fierce grace, again, was inviting me to spiritual transformation.

Throughout my conversation with Jesus during this January 2016 direction session, he kept encouraging me to put my old expectations down. He asked me quite pointedly "What if I want something different for you?" It had never occurred to me that God might be providing me with a different option apart from biological children. But at this juncture in my prayer with Jesus, it seemed he was doing just that. Jesus reminded me that if he had followed the "normal" Jewish thing (go back to his family and be the responsible eldest son instead of traveling around in ministry), he wouldn't have fulfilled his call. Cultural expectations are decidedly overrated. Bazinga!

Thanks to this prayer time with Jesus, I was able to hold my desire for children loosely enough to actually let the desire fall out of my hands and lay on the ground. I had been carrying this desire for a very long time, and I was relieved to finally let it go. In my mind's eye during the prayer, these dreams and expectations turned to ash as I left them behind. I walked away from the ashes, ready to hold whatever new thing God had in store for me.

Women's Bodies, [Re]Production and Cultural Captivity

As Jesus continues to remind me, cultural expectations are overrated. But they're like the air we breathe and aren't visible or even recognized as something unhealthy and potentially oppressive. I grew up in the affluent suburbs of Detroit and Philadelphia with achievement-oriented parents. My parents raised me with the belief that I could do anything I put my mind to, all I had to do was work hard and follow through. They raised me to own my actions, be self-sufficient, and not short change myself. They didn't blink when I said I wanted to be an engineer, they believed my gender had nothing to do with my career choice.

Yet culture had wormed its way into my beliefs about myself in ways that reduced my identity as a strong, capable, intelligent woman with gifts and graces. Magazines and television told me I needed to be pretty and supplied hundreds of photos indicating what ideal beauty looked like. Advertising told me that I needed X, Y, and Z and that I was incomplete if I didn't achieve, buy, or have whatever it was they were selling. Christian circles and well-meaning friends sometimes accidentally and often intentionally told me that my value was based on how well my womb did its job. After all, the Bible says that we're only here to reproduce (please note my sarcasm). Patriarchy tells me that my beliefs, intelligence, voice, and body don't matter because I have ovaries instead of testes.

Somehow, unintentionally, I came to internalize these beliefs, and these false narratives were killing me, or at least giving me serious joint pain and stiffness. Fierce grace had been doing everything in her power to get my attention. It took six months for me to willingly admit the real issue and then bring it to God for us to unpack. When I woke up the next day (after my direction session with Mindy in January 2016) I had no random pain or stiffness at all, and I haven't had any since. This is just another reminder to me that my body, thanks to fierce grace, is often wiser than my mind admits.

Fierce grace pointed out that the maddening thing for me about all of this is that culturally speaking, much of my value as a woman is still placed in whether I have a husband and have produced children. One of the first questions I get asked when I meet new people is "Do you have kids?" I understand that this question is asked to make conversation because most people love talking about their kids, but I don't have any to talk about. The follow up question when I respond "No, I don't have kids" is sometimes "Would you like to have kids?" My negative answer of "Not at this point in life" occasionally makes people visibly uncomfortable. Some people try to encourage me and say things like "Well you're not too old yet" or "It's not too late." The snarky person in me wants to respond, "Yeah, yeah. Whatever. You just met me. What makes you think you have the right to give me advice on whether I should continue trying to having children?" But now I respond with something benign like "My husband and I have other interests that we're pursuing, and children don't fit in the picture anymore." People are often surprised at this very specific articulation of the lack of desire. It's like they think I'm going to lament or be sad because my sole purpose as a woman cannot be fulfilled, or, even worse, that something is wrong with me because I'm not sad or lamenting my lack of children.

At one point several years ago I was miserable because I so desperately wanted children. I. Wanted. Children. I'd love to blame my misery completely on cultural expectations, but it's not true. The interweaving of cultural expectations and my desire for children set the stage for supreme disappointment. The culture was telling me that I'm less valuable if I don't reproduce. I wanted children and, for whatever reason, my body refused. I remember sitting in the sanctuary of my church, talking to a woman who hadn't had biological children but married a man later in life who had children and grandchildren. I was weeping because I couldn't believe how much I longed for and missed something that I hadn't had. There was no getting around it. I had to walk through the pain.

And the world (especially the conservative Christian world) likes to heap shame on people and pity them when a couple is experiencing infertility, which is why Pat and I kept our issues private for so long. The shame and pity story is similar to listening to Job's friends. "I'm so sorry you haven't been able to have children. Have you looked at your life and determined if sin is keeping you from reproducing?" Like an inability to reproduce is because of a woman's sin. Not my husband's, but my sin. Wow. That's screwed up and not at all scriptural. Yes, I understand that it is written in the beginning God created male and female and told them to populate the earth. But reproduction is not our primary purpose; reproduction is not the female's primary purpose. Our (both males' and females') primary purpose, that which fulfills us and encourages our true selves to shine through, is to be in a healthy and whole relationship with God, ourselves, other people, and creation. Our primary purpose may or may not include biological reproduction, and fierce grace has helped me see this.

A Complicated Scriptural History

As 2018 began, fierce grace prompted me to do a blitz read (a super-fast and intense reading) of the Bible, so I read through the Bible in approximately 46 days. It is a lot of reading but doing this practice every so often has been very beneficial for my spiritual life. During this blitz read, I noticed patterns and beliefs that seemed to be acceptable to the biblical writers (like patriarchy mixed with war, power struggles, and genocide). Today, many people don't like reading the Old Testament specifically because of the war, genocide, and disregard for women and the marginalized, which is understandable. Fierce grace showed me that our culture has significantly changed in many ways, yet patriarchy and its ramifications still impact both church and societal systems. I define patriarchy as a system of repression that devalues all other narratives besides that of the ethnic majority male.

We don't have to get very far in the first book of the Bible, Genesis, to see that both men and women see the value of a woman by her ability to produce male children. Now, for a nomadic tribe like Abraham's, this in some ways made sense because more boys means more workers (and more fighters/defenders of the tribe), and a man biologically cannot bring a human being into this world by carrying it in his non-existent uterus for nine-ish months.

But this ability to bring life into the world was both a blessing and a curse for women. It seems that many women (at least in the Old Testament) are mentioned in no small part because of their children. Women like Sarah (Genesis 12-23), Rachel (Genesis 29-35), and Hannah (1 Samuel 1-2), are three women that come to mind who were not able to conceive for a while and are mentioned specifically in the Bible. They seem to have the same story...their husbands love them with or without children, but their husbands also have other wives or slaves that can bear sons. Sarah, Rachel, and Hannah are tormented by the other women in their husbands' lives because they cannot conceive, and at times, it is unbearable. Eventually they are all able to bear at least one son, passing on the legacy of God's promise to Abraham from one generation to the next. This genealogy was very important to the Israelites because it linked them back to Abraham, the father of the Jewish faith. We even see this male lineage being highlighted in the Gospel according to Matthew, even though scripture tells us that Joseph had nothing to do with Jesus' conception. Unfortunately, a surficial reading of the Old Testament can leave us with the misconception that God believes women aren't valuable for other things besides carrying on the family legacy through childbearing.

Yet as I did my blitz read and moved into the New Testament, I was surprised by what fierce grace was showing me. Jesus repeatedly broke every societal and religious norm regarding the treatment of and interaction with women. There are several examples in the gospels where Jesus spoke to women directly and in public, which went against Jewish custom (women were to barely be seen and never heard or acknowledged). The story of the Samaritan woman at the well is a great example (John 4, one of my favorite stories about Jesus). Jesus had a very interesting conversation with the woman, and fierce grace showed me that it brought him joy. I noticed that he treated her respectfully, answered her questions, and didn't disregard her concerns and confusion. She was not in any way discounted or demeaned because of her womanhood (or her five "husbands").

Fierce grace challenged me to look more seriously at Jesus' life and ministry. What tables would Jesus overturn today? What limitations have we placed on ourselves and others that have no place when following Jesus? If Christians believe that Jesus is the incarnation and embodiment of God, then we should take our cues from him in how we treat others even if society and/or Church are giving us a conflicting message. Jesus broke the mold as a Jewish man, and maybe we should too (more on this in chapter six!).

Even though Jesus was such a boundary crusher when it came to women's dignity and value, Paul's letters have unfortunately been a source of oppression and limitation for women. For example, the New Testament includes two of Paul's letters to Timothy, a young leader in the Gentile church. In 1 Timothy 2:12 Paul very specifically tells Timothy that no wife (or woman) should teach a man. This particular scripture passage has caused great debate when it comes to the ordination of women in the Church. Yet in the verses immediately before Paul's direction for women to be silent, he says that women should also dress modestly and not braid their hair or wear expensive jewelry or clothing. Seems like we're practicing selective literalism with Paul's letter to Timothy: verse twelve is to be taken literally but verses nine and ten don't apply anymore. Really? I'm certain I've never been chastised as being ungodly for braiding my hair or wearing a gold necklace. In contrast, I have been treated differently as a clergywoman when I preach or teach because of this passage in 1 Timothy 2:12.

It wasn't until I got to seminary that I heard the term "occasional" (used in reference to Paul's letters during a hermeneutics class). This term, "occasional," indicates that the Epistles (and some other books of the Bible depending on your interpretation of scripture) were written to a specific group of people at a certain time in history and answered questions to which we don't have access. We only have half the story. This specificity then dramatically limits our ability to universally apply the letter's suggestions and advice. Paul wrote to Timothy knowing that Timothy was leading a group of Gentiles who met in each other's homes. There was a very defined order to how a Greek household was run, and a woman teaching a group of people (including men) in a home would have been considered disrespectful. Paul's advice to Timothy was more about keeping order in the Greek household in the first century than it was about whether women, at any time in the future, should be ordained to lead churches.

Reflecting on my journey, I see that fierce grace has been urging me to understand scripture in a way that brings honor to all creation. If we as twenty-first century Christians don't consider and understand the cultural context and "occasions" of the Bible and its writings, we can mistakenly devalue half of humanity. Based on my journey and experience I see that fierce grace has encouraged me to let go of a literal interpretation of scripture and the certainty that it provides. Fierce grace has strongly prompted me to lean into and use my strengths as a woman, even if some people think it goes against the Bible.

The Myths Continue

In addition to doing the blitz read of scripture at the beginning of 2018, fierce grace prompted me to take a hard look at how women are treated and perceived in society. What made me incredibly frustrated from fierce grace's nudge was that I saw how women are still considered expendable and consumable. Women are seen as objects to be won or conquered, subjugated and controlled, not valued nor treasured, not respected nor honored for the unique gifts we have as women and individuals.

Women's bodies (our beings even) are not our own from a very young age. We are taught that being physically desirable is more important than intelligence, strength, or tenacity. We are taught that if we don't meet the ideal specifications (whatever that may be at the time), then we are worthless. We are taught that we exist for other people's pleasure. We are taught to be nice, pleasing, pretty, and not too smart (we wouldn't want to intimidate men with our intelligence, would we? That's not at all nice or pleasing). When I was in eleventh grade, my brother, who was in seventh grade, said to me, "Karen, you're never going to find a man until you learn to keep your mouth shut." I still think this is funny, but for very different reasons. I was and still am an incredibly opinionated person and tend to share my opinion more than might be appreciated by those around me. But Les was right; many men want someone to support them, to be their cheerleader, to tell them how great they are even when they are awful human beings.

[As an aside, there's a song by Omi called "Cheerleader" that I despised the moment it came out. The lyrics talk about how happy he is because he has a girl who is his cheerleader and is *always* supportive of him. Even now the song still makes me want to throat punch the dude who wrote it. I'm not your mama, I'm not your cheerleader, and I'm not June Cleaver.]

There is also this cultural myth that a woman will wait for her man for whatever reason. I don't like to wait for anyone, male or female. Pat knew from the beginning that I wasn't going to be the average girlfriend. (He likes to say I'm a lot to handle. I like to say I keep him on his toes.) When we graduated from college and he hadn't yet decided what he was going to do with his life, I asked him very pointedly what his intentions were regarding our relationship (it was 2001 and we had been together for three plus years). He said that he thought getting married in 2010 would be a good time. Nine years...I about blew a gasket. I told him in no uncertain terms that if we weren't married by the end of 2003, then he was out, and we were done. I wasn't going to wait around for someone for ten years to decide if he wanted to marry me. I could find someone else if necessary. Pat was stunned. I can't even imagine the conversation he had with our friends about this. It makes me laugh just thinking about it, and I'm amazed I actually said it out loud. It was brazen even for me. But one of our friends asked me a few months later about the conversation. He wanted to verify that I said these things because he couldn't believe it. He knew that Pat wouldn't lie, but apparently my view on the subject was not what he expected. I laughed and responded, "Hell yeah I said it. I'm not waiting around for someone who doesn't want to commit to me. 2010? Are you serious? That's just flat out ridiculous."

Granted, my extreme independence was on full display in the second story about Pat and me, but I think that these examples display the cultural norms for women and for relationships between women and men. It was very out of the ordinary that I, a female, was completely content in finding my own path, of supporting myself, of being hyper-self-reliant, of living life very clearly on my terms. I didn't need a guy to fulfill me or to complete my life. Fierce grace has shown me that my hyper-independence in my early and mid-twenties came from a place of brokenness. As I've said, my self-reliance can be pathological. Because of fierce grace's action in my life, I've been healed enough to be able to live into my independent spirit in new ways that are more holistic. For example, because of fierce grace I see more clearly the systemic injustice against women in the United States and am an advocate for women specifically through my spiritual direction and coaching practice, which is much different than the selfish independence I displayed over fifteen years ago.

Back to Enough

Fierce grace has made it very clear that I am enough as a woman, regardless of whether I produce children. Every once in a while, when Pat and I are around people our age with older children I think, "Holy cow! I could have a fifteen-year-old. That's disturbing." It turns out I can be my true self, I can be enough in my innate womanhood without biological children. As I evaluate my journey so far at forty, I am reminded of one of the more interesting things about my conversation with Mindy and Jesus in January 2016. Jesus and I talked about whether or not God wanted me to have children and what this meant for me as a woman. His invitation has come true in a few ways. Jesus was inviting me to focus not on biological children but spiritual children. Through my direction and coaching practice I have eleven spiritual children who I am able to help see God in ways they would never have expected. I ask them questions about their spiritual growth, their relationships with God, their work, and families. I get to journey with people through the hard things of life such as loss, grief, illness, change, the unknown, the gut-wrenching, and the terrifying. As I walk alongside people I have the privilege of seeing them grow in love and change in spectacularly beautiful ways.

This life that I'm living into is enough for me. I am grateful that fierce grace has been working in my life to get me to appreciate my (and others') value as a woman and that I see her fingerprints in this aspect of my life. However, my identity isn't the only thing fierce grace has been working on. She has shown up to meddle in some other ways that I've been formed by scripture, including how I understand who God is and what the Divine eternally wants for us.

Chapter 7

Hold It Loosely: Heaven, Hell, & God-Images

I've heard several people say that the work of adulthood is the unlearning of false ideologies and unhealthy behavior patterns we picked up as children. I give a strong "Yes indeed!" to this sentiment. I picked up so many behavior patterns as a kid that became extremely unhealthy in adulthood. For me, self-reliance is the primary roadblock to my physical, mental, emotional, and spiritual well-being. I've been unlearning the extreme version of self-reliance for eight years, and I think I've finally turned the corner where I don't believe that I need to be superhuman anymore. Yes, I fall in to traps of old behavior patterns, but I'm catching myself more and more quickly.

This same thing is also happening to my understanding of God. The faith that we were taught as children was simplistic for a very good reason: children's brains are not fully developed. This limits a child's capacity for reason, comprehension, impulse control, etc. For those of us who grew up going to Sunday school, we learned simple truths about God that have stayed with us for much of our lives.

However, fierce grace has shown me that some of the ideas I acquired as a child haven't been helpful as an adult, and I know that this is the case with many others as well. As I taught Bible Study with my three churches over the year of my interim pastoral appointment, we talked a lot about beliefs and why we have them. During our Heaven and Hell study several participants made comments about certain things they believed about the afterlife and what Jesus said about eternity. When I stopped the conversation and asked, "Where and when did you learn that?" Most of the time the answer was "at home" or "in church" and "when I was a kid." I asked if what people had told them was in the Bible, and they didn't know. They believed what their parents or pastors told them because these people were adults and could be trusted. Keep in mind that the people in this study were in their sixties, if not older. They had carried many of these ideas for at least five decades.

The most common thing that I heard was that people were looking forward to seeing their relatives again. They expected to be welcomed to heaven by their parents or grandparents or whoever was important to them, like when you complete a race and there are people cheering for you at the finish line. Maybe I'm incredibly unsentimental or crass, but I don't give a rip if when I die my grandparents or parents (if they die before me) meet me in heaven. I'd be affronted because they aren't Jesus. I don't want Peter at the pearly gates or Paul or Deborah or Ruth or my Grandad or Pap-pap or Grandma. If there are pearly gates, I want Jesus to meet me.

When I said this to my cadre of older people at Bible study, most of them were horrified. The looks on their faces were priceless. They were disturbed in some respects because they interpreted these comments as me saying that I don't love my family, which is entirely untrue. My love for my family is representative of my love for Jesus, but my relationship with Jesus is my highest priority, more than my love for my family (and btw, this is scriptural, see Luke 14:26). After they got over the shock, they realized that maybe I had a point. Some of them even laughed. Why would family meeting me in heaven be more important than having Jesus meet me and say, "Well done good and faithful servant?" I'm an Enneagram Type One, I want to know that I lived my life "right" after all. And what better affirmation of that is there besides Jesus meeting me to tell me I didn't screw up completely?

We don't know what happens after death, no matter how hard we try, no matter how many times we read books on heaven written by people who come back from the dead. Even though we might have the best of intentions to bring others comfort and consolation, I'm not convinced telling someone that their loved one is smiling down on them and watching over them is the best choice. Remarks like these bring certainty, which offers comfort, but for whom? The consolations we offer may be ways that we're trying to bring control or order into the messy world of emotions because we're the ones who are uncomfortable with expressed grief. I wonder if sitting in silence with people; helping them honor their pain yet not trying to explain away the suffering; and reminding them of the love shared is a more wholistic choice. Since fierce grace is present in our loss and our confusion about the afterlife, I'm thinking that holding these ideas loosely could allow for fierce grace's transformative work in our lives.

During the same study on a different night, we talked about the historical evolution of the afterlife. We looked at the Old Testament and the Jews' lack of discussion about it. We looked at the New Testament and Jesus' parable about Lazarus and the Rich Man (see Luke 16: 19-31). We discussed how Jesus often used familiar imagery to get a very explicit point across. However, the use of this specific imagery doesn't necessarily make it literal since Jesus spoke in parables most of the time. My Bible study peeps weren't all that impressed with this discussion either.

They wanted a definitive heaven and hell, a right and a wrong, and a reward and a punishment. They were comfortable with the certainty of believing in a heaven and hell. They were uncomfortable with the potential unknown if scripture wasn't literal. They desired a controlled outcome: if I do such and such, then I will get rewarded in heaven. I can't fault them for that, since most of them grew up being told that you need to believe in and work hard for God so you can go to heaven.

Fierce grace has helped me see a distinct lack of spiritual freedom in this viewpoint of hard work to receive eternal reward. By the time I led this study, fierce grace had upended my frame of reference on this issue. Through my research and compilation of material, I realized that no matter what I believe about the afterlife, my belief doesn't impact what actually happens. I can believe there's a heaven and hell, and I can believe that my work earns me a spot in heaven. Yet it doesn't make it true. It seems like a lot of hard work and slogging, which is the opposite of Jesus' message about taking his "easy" yoke. Our understanding of the afterlife is fraught with pitfalls, potholes, and serious uncertainty. It's messy, and no matter how I try, I can't control the outcome of what happens to me after death. The various eternal options discussed in scripture may be accurate and true, but I personally can't hold these ideas as central tenets of my faith. It seems that I'm not alone in this, because telling people that they need to believe in Jesus so they go to heaven and don't go to hell is no longer a compelling message for many. A lot of people don't believe there is a place after we die, let alone one of eternal fire and punishment (Thanks for the nightmares, Dante).

Since I had wrestled with this issue and came to an undefined resolution of sorts, my goal for the Bible study was to get people thinking about what they believe, why they believe it, and where their beliefs actually come from so that they could do the same thing (regardless of whether they came to the same spot in their understanding). Fierce grace was using me to loosen the group's grip on certainty regarding this issue, and I enjoyed the back and forth, the discussion, the expressed frustration, and the laughter. In spite of not having certainty, we all felt Jesus there in the midst of our conversations.

Praise Jesus, one of the ladies in the group received what I was sharing and was willing to verbalize her takeaways from the study. Keep in mind that this woman in her sixties was born and raised Roman Catholic and never studied the Bible. When I arrived at the church in July, she had just read through the Bible for the first time at the beginning of the year. There was a lot she was interested in learning, and she had some great questions. (I loved her questions because they made me think too!) At the end of our four-week study, she remarked that she was surprised at how much stuff she had learned growing up that wasn't from the Bible; that she wanted to hold these ideas lightly because we don't know for certain; and she realized that she isn't so incredibly worried about what happens after death anymore. I'm pretty sure I cheered after she said this. Her realization was the whole point of me going through this topic with them. We don't know. We can't say for certain, and maybe we should hold these ideas a bit looser.

Another thing fierce grace pointed out to me as I worked on this study was that eternal life has been used as this carrot to get people to conform to a certain set of behavioral standards as dictated by the church. In reality, a more literal interpretation of Jesus' comments on heaven and hell might actually not matter so much as our relationship with Christ, which is what really has the power to transform our attitudes and behaviors through fierce grace. I say this because I believe that our eternal life (and participation in God's kingdom) starts the moment we are conceived. We have so many glorious opportunities to participate in co-laboring and co-creating with God here and now, if we're paying attention to fierce grace's nudges. This participation isn't something to be nonchalant about. Jesus was pretty clear with his disciples and other followers that the reign of heaven started with his coming to the world and starting his ministry, and *all people* are invited to participate. Jesus gives us a constant invitation to participate in the kingdom of God while we are here on earth. Our reward, if you want to call it that, is through and because of our relationship with Jesus. We are rewarded in this life with the gift of transformation, with the fruit of the Spirit, with an easy yoke because of Jesus' love and fierce grace's action in our lives.

Fierce grace invites us to experience God's joy and love here and now, in the midst of the suffering we see all around us. We, in this life, spiritually reap what we spiritually sow. If I live a life focused on Christ now, then whether or not there is a heaven immediately ready to receive me when I die is almost irrelevant in my mind. I got to know Jesus imperfectly during my lifetime, and I think God is okay with that. Knowing Jesus now is its own beautiful and messy reward. We don't have to wait until we die to be flooded with Jesus' love, grace, compassion, and mercy. We can experience it here in this lifetime and are invited to do so by fierce grace.

More False Ideology: God Images

As fierce grace was tweaking my understanding of eternal life, she was also bringing awareness to an idea I had of God that wasn't a good fit anymore. Somewhere along the line I acquired the idea that Creator God (a.k.a. God "the

Father") was a muscular old man with long hair and a scepter who didn't want me to do what I wanted to do and could get very angry when I was disobedient. Think of a combination of the Sistine Chapel God and Ariel's father, King Triton, in *The Little Mermaid* Disney animated film. For a long time, I was subconsciously afraid of this God withholding his love from me, and this image was representative of that fear. Let me be clear that this is not a healthy image of Creator God. I cognitively knew that my picture of God was inaccurate, but I still acted like it was true. (Generally, I'm an image/tactile person, so pictures and images tend to stay with me longer than can be healthy.)

Fierce grace recognized that I was struggling with this image of God the Father and was happy to jump in to help with my transformation. She knew that me working through this dissonance would increase my spiritual freedom and was eager to facilitate the growth. Looking back, it was like she exclaimed, "Yippee! Another way Karen is growing and transforming in Christ. Let's do this!" As is my way, I brought this struggle to spiritual direction because it had bothered me for longer than forty-eight hours. In talking with my spiritual direction supervisor, Bill, we went back and forth about how I know the King Triton image is untrue, but I have no other image of who God is. Bill asked me a very simple and direct question: "What happens if that image goes away and there's no need to replace it?" All at once it occurred to me that this question was inviting me to freedom, and I leapt at the chance. "Poof!" And away my god-image went. It never occurred to me that I could be in relationship with an imageless God. Fierce grace, in speaking through Bill, provided the option for an imageless deity, and it was such a liberation! It was like a weight had been lifted from my shoulders, and my soul and body felt much lighter. I left this unhealthy image behind and didn't feel compelled to create a new one. Creator God didn't need to have a form, and it was an amazing and blessed relief.

This image of God as a tyrant (or at least a hard, demanding, and imposing God) is amazingly pervasive in the circles in which I mingle. Granted, I live in central PA, so people here have been pretty conservative for a long time. There's also a strong puritanical influence that is compounded by Germanic heritage that expects hard work at any cost. People affirm that they don't need to do anything to earn God's love and then in the same breath they lament how no one is willing to work anymore or volunteer for this committee or bring their kids to Sunday school. I realize there's a whole bunch of different ideas at play in these conversations, but there is this expectation that God requires us to work hard and sacrifice ourselves for him. (Generally, I think Jesus would disagree. While on tour, Jesus didn't hustle for anyone, even his dead friend Lazarus. Remember the ladies remarking that their brother would be stinky by now if they opened up the tomb? See John 11.)

This image of God as tyrant plays into an unhealthy compulsion to ignore self-care, to be super busy, and to wear it like a badge of honor. I have fallen prey to all of this at a very high cost to my physical and emotional well-being. It is not surprising to me that my ideas about the faux Creator God were crumbling as I was recovering from a very unhealthy 2015. I was working three different jobs and burning the candle from both ends and the middle. I had fallen into the trap that if I just worked harder then things would be okay. I had zero understanding of what it was to honor myself, and I went down in flaming wreckage.

At the strongly worded suggestions of my close friends, I scheduled another appointment with Dr. Rocket after my panic attack in November 2015. I wanted to find out once and for all how I could stop spiraling into an anxiety-ridden abyss. Twice was quite enough. I'll never forget what he told me. Dr. Rocket looked at me and said in no uncertain terms that I needed to learn how to say "no" and mean it. THE HORROR! This was not the advice I was expecting, yet he was dead serious. At one point in my life, my twenties, I had been really good at saying no. And then something happened, and I honestly don't know what it was. Somewhere along the way I made the choice to put other people's wants ahead of my own needs, and it was destroying me from the inside out. Dr. Rocket gave me the permission I needed to honor and take care of myself, and with that permission I had to re-learn how to say no to both God and people.

Saying no to God might sound weird to some of you. You might be thinking, "Saying no to God? Isn't that against the Jesus code? Won't I be disobedient if I tell God no?" Nope. It's not, you won't. Saying no to God isn't even on the list for heresy (if there is such a thing), especially when the god we're saying no to is a tyrant or slave-master. That god that we're working so hard for will never be satisfied, will not take no for an answer, and nothing we do will ever be good enough. This tyrant god is not God, it's an idol or false god we've created on our own or adopted along our journey. And we're supposed to say no to this god.

Now saying no to tyrant god took some additional energy on my part, because I re-evaluated everything that I thought God had said to me or asked me to do in the last three years. I realized that I was carrying around a lot of garbage that really needed to be thrown out, which is how I ended up talking with Bill about tyrant god and having tyrant god go "Poof!" He wasn't helpful or life-giving, so he needed to go.

Saying no to God also meant saying no to people. This reevaluation process included many things that left me uncomfortable. I felt like I was going back on my word, which is something I don't do. If I make a commitment, by god, I'll be seeing it through (hear the dysfunction yet? It's so beautiful!). I reexamined my jobs and what I thought God thought of them, which meant quitting one and taking a hiatus from another. I backed out of as many obligations as possible and asked others to take over what couldn't be cancelled. Hear me people: this was incredibly hard for me, but I knew with every ounce of my being that I needed to learn what it meant to honor my body and emotions and treat myself with dignity. This task was so difficult for me that I had my Waterworks Advisory Board focus singularly on holding me accountable for my self-care for two years because I knew I would take on more than was healthy if left to my own devices. I needed people to be truth-tellers in my life, even if it hurt.

In the spring of 2017, I had another conversation with Mindy about God stuff. During this conversation about Creator God, the old image of King Triton popped in my head. Mindy encouraged me to go to God in prayer and explore why this image came back to me. I closed my eyes, and mentally pictured my old image of God the Father. I asked Jesus what he wanted me to see, and immediately the King Triton god-image turned into a giant gold hand that shook its finger at me as if to say, "No, no, no. Don't you remember? This image is gone. This is not who I am." Through this imagery, fierce grace was reminding me of my transformation and keeping me on the path. As soon as I sensed this message, I envisioned the hand disintegrating into thousands of shiny gold foil confetti pieces that surrounded me and were part of me at the same time. This was a surprise. As I sat with this image for several days after my direction session, I pondered the significance of the shift in understanding. At one point, I had an image of the gold confetti permeating all living things as a reminder that there might be more to human beings (and life in general) created in the likeness of God than strictly our capacity for good. Fierce grace was getting me to acknowledge that there might be something more to our physical selves than that for which I have given God credit. There may be more to the world than I have been willing to acknowledge. There is a divine imprint on everything in this world and fierce grace was helping me experience the wonder of this divine imprint.

As Rob Bell would say, "Everything is spiritual." This is the message that I received very strongly from fierce grace and have since turned into a spiritual practice. I began to wonder about the world and God, to discover a sense of wonder in the rustling of leaves, with the quick glimpses of our yard bunnies and birds, and with the feeling of the sun on my face. Even the simple act of sitting with a friend for coffee has inspired wonder and deep gratitude in me. There's a wonder and a beauty to everything around us if we're willing to be open to it. I've noticed that this shift in contemplation has changed how I interact with the world and the reverence and awe I have for it. Because of fierce grace's resolve in transforming my life, I now feel relationally connected to the earth, like it's a part of my family, like the grass and the trees and the chipmunks that sound alarms at my presence are all part of my family.

Fierce grace has opened me up to a deep appreciation that is very reminiscent of St. Francis of Assisi's poem Brother Sun...I looked at the world and said, "Thank you for showing God to me in a different way. Thank you for unceasingly being who you have been created to be to give me an example of how God is inviting me to live. Thank you for living with humans in spite of all the damage we do." There's a gratefulness, love, and honoring spirit within me that can be overwhelming at times. And to the chipmunk that was feverishly chirping at me this morning as I stood outside of camp enjoying the unseasonably warm, fresh morning air I said, "We're family. You don't need to sound the alarm, I won't be hurting you. Seriously. Calm down." This chipmunk was intense. I decided to go inside since I seemed to be causing it serious anxiety. My "gift" to the chipmunk.

For me, allowing fierce grace to help me let go of old ideas and god-images has led to an expanding interior freedom, which manifests in a deeper appreciation for the universe God created. This appreciation could be for myself, a specific person, creation, etc. When the heavy but invisible ties of false ideas dissolve, it makes room for an inner spaciousness and freedom that I couldn't have orchestrated. These times are surprising, subversive, and radical. They leap out of my blind spots with intensity and strength, gentleness and love. When these moments show up in spiritual direction, Mindy has remarked in various ways, "This is definitely God at work in you because you wouldn't have gone here in a million years." Nope, I couldn't have created this situation in ten million years. This is all fierce grace at work, and I wouldn't have it any other way.

Fortunately for us, fierce grace doesn't rest on her laurels. My ideas about heaven, hell, eternal life, and God the Father weren't the only ideas she wanted to transform. My views about personal hypocrisy, what constitutes heresy, and the purpose of prayer landed on her cutting board in the late summer of 2018.

Chapter 8

Hypocrisy & Heresy World

Imagine this…you're sitting in worship on the second Sunday of the month and you're invited to sing the Apostles' Creed. In terms of creeds, I have considered it fairly benign. There's not much weird Greek philosophy verbiage used like in the Nicene Creed, it's pretty straight-forward, and it's succinct. Yet, as I sat there, I noticed this growing discomfort in my body. I felt a strong resistance to singing any of the Apostles' Creed, especially the middle section about Jesus being born of a virgin named Mary. (If you don't know the Apostles' Creed, now is the time to google it.) By the end of the song, I wanted to run out of the sanctuary screaming. I had this strange and physical realization that maybe, just maybe, the Apostles' Creed wasn't true and that it didn't communicate Truth. Maybe it was somehow lying to us and so were the people who wrote it. The horror. "Have I been believing the wrong thing all this time?" I wondered. Later in the service, we said the Lord's Prayer (using trespasses of course, because why would we actually call something sin?), and I had a hard time with that too. During the worship service, I ended up writing my own version of the Lord's Prayer that felt more authentic to who I was at the moment, one that was a bit less focused on form and more open to the Spirit (at least I thought so).

So, as the spiritual director that I am, I started wondering about my reaction and asking myself direction questions. I asked myself "What was it about the Creed that triggered this violent revulsion?" What I received in response was more angst in my body. And I didn't have the time to sit with it very much between my noticing the repulsion on Sunday morning and my spiritual direction session the next evening. So, I brought my angst to Mindy. She has this innate and distinctly alarming cultivated power of perception that cuts to the heart of any matter. She also doesn't let me get away with bullshit. I appreciate that.

I told her that I had taken issue with the Apostles' Creed, and I was concerned that I had crossed over into the interesting, if frightening and ever-changing, Heresy World. Since starting seminary I've vacationed in Heresy World regularly (Origen and Pelagius really aren't so terrible. I still think Marcion missed the entire point of the Hebrew Bible.). Heresy World is not a bad place, really. In fact, it helps me clarify what I believe and why I believe it, which is incredibly useful. Heresy World is a great place to visit and if you haven't been there, take a spiritual director friend and fierce grace and see what it's like. You might notice some new things about your faith and what is deeply important to you because of fierce grace's invitation. I think she likes to give out tickets to Heresy World, it might be her personal playground if she has such a thing. When I accept fierce grace's invitation and enter Heresy World, I'm never quite sure of what kind of experience awaits. I don't know if it will be the torture of the Disney "It's a Small World" ride, a desert wasteland, or a luxury spa retreat. But the vacation with fierce grace in Heresy World is always worth it. However, these trips do make me a bit nervous since I'm an ordained UM deacon, and I took a vow to uphold the UMC Book of Discipline, which is SO via media that it hurts at times.

During direction, Mindy and I talked, laughed, clarified, fell silent, discerned, noticed, and reflected. And we ended up taking a path that led to my heart opening to Love in such a way that I left some, but not all, judgment of the Apostles' Creed behind. In an unsatisfying way during this direction session, I experienced God telling me that the form (of prayer, of affirmation, of worship) is less important than the desire of the people to grow closer to God. God is happy, if we can anthropomorphize God for a moment, when people are gathered in relationship that increases their capacity to love. I only half bought it and told God that we would discuss it later.

I moved on. Sort of. I continued to remind myself when I didn't like a form of something that God didn't take offense, so I shouldn't either. But my internal angst was affirmed and given voice through my continued reading of *Insurrection* by Peter Rollins. There is something to be said for reading books that knock traditional theology off balance in a way that invites wholeness, spiritual freedom, and an increase of love.

Jesus and the Status Quo

As I continued reflecting on the Apostles' Creed and becoming Christ-like through fierce grace's invitations to Heresy World, I was struck by the fact that Jesus was a seriously out-of-the-box thinker. He was a Jewish heretic who defied all kinds of cultural norms and who thumbed his nose at the traditional interpretations of the Torah. The Pharisees or Sadducees or scribes or teachers of the law were always getting on Jesus' case because of the way he presented his understanding of God and our relationships with God and others.

There's the section in the Gospel of Mark where Jesus was questioned by the Pharisees about divorce. Jesus told the Pharisees that Moses allowed people to get divorced because their hearts were hard, but God had a more unifying and holistic plan for creation (Mark 10:2-12). The Pharisees also had a fit over Jesus allowing his disciples to pick grain on the Sabbath (Mark 2:23-28). Jesus responded that the Sabbath was made for man, not the other way around. In the Gospel of Luke, a Pharisee noticed that Jesus didn't wash his hands before eating according to the Jewish custom. Jesus then embarked on a "woe to you" message that told them how they were too concerned with outward appearances and should be concerned with justice, mercy, and generosity (Luke 11:37-53). One of the teachers of the law even told Jesus that he was insulting them. This was funny, 'cause Jesus didn't care.

We can read these passages and sometimes think that we should be the crusaders telling the world how they are wrong. Not so much, at least not in the way we see demonstrated today, especially online. The culture of Facebook and Twitter doesn't often help us become reflective or discerning when it comes to how we live our lives, what comes out of our mouths, and who we say it to. So many planks in eyes on Facebook, including my own. However, after we get past Jesus giving the Jewish hyper-religious folk the what-for, there's some other message that Jesus is communicating. This message is one of generosity, love, and kindness, which goes against the rituals, customs, and law-enforcing nature of the Jewish hierarchy. Jesus is reinterpreting-much of the Hebrew Scriptures, and it makes the people in power very nervous, angry even.[1]

---

[1] For a good book on signs and symbols and how they change, read Crystal Downing's book *Changing Signs of Truth* (Downers Grove, IL: IVP Academic, 2012). It is a text book, so don't be surprised at the specifics and detail included. But it's a helpful read if you're into the study of language and semiotics.

It seems like followers of Jesus are often called to rethink how the gospel is shared and interpreted. Over the last two-thousand years, the Christian faith has gone through a myriad of changes, not the least being the parting between the Orthodox and Catholic Churches, the Protestant Reformation, and the vast number of different religious orders that have popped up throughout history (Jesuits, Franciscans, and Benedictines come immediately to mind). Each of these changes within the body of Christ signaled an invitation to reach people in new ways, much to the dismay of those in authority. Today there's a radical reforming happening around race, religion, gender, and status. The old ways of being aren't holding water anymore. Our messaging and programming need to change. We must find different ways of conveying the gospel so that it is compelling, relatable, and meaningful to those both inside and outside the church.

So, what is fierce grace inviting us to do or become? I think we are being invited to become heretics and out-of-the-box thinkers like Jesus, if we can stomach the tension. Some of us need to become boundary pushers in our own traditions so that we can reach more of the world with true transformation through Jesus Christ. As I mentioned earlier, some people are completely okay with believing what other people tell them and staying inside the box. We need those types of people in society and the church. But for other people such as myself (the Enneagram Type One "Reformer" along with Ignatius of Loyola, Paul, and John Wesley), we tend to see the world as an improvement project and the status quo box as a problem to be solved.

Maintaining the status quo generally only benefits those that are in power (ahem, patriarchy) and/or those who like the status quo and the rules that go with them. Admittedly, the boundaries of the status quo bring many people a sense of comfort, especially when they're on the inside. Comfort isn't necessarily a bad thing, but when it comes at the cost of excluding or alienating others and pushes people away from Jesus, we should probably reevaluate our religious choices. The rules (and those who feel the need to enforce them) keep the established patterns and behaviors as norms, which may not be what's currently needed in our world. Unfortunately, those on the margins are automatically excluded from the status quo because they don't fit in the box and cannot, for whatever reason, conform to the rules. Yet Jesus hung out with the "sinners" on the margins and didn't think twice about it. After all, Jesus is the one who invited himself to have dinner with Zacchaeus, the chief tax collector of Jericho (see Luke 19:1-10).

In my work with churches, it always surprises me that even a whiff of change makes many people nervous. After all, the status quo wouldn't be the status quo if it changed. We would be forced to rethink our policies and procedures and signs and symbols. People would be uncomfortable. It's not "nice" or "pleasing" to think this way. At the same time, sometimes we need a boot in our ass to help us realize that we aren't awesome. Sometimes that boot is covered in daisies with sunshine radiating from it, but not all the time. Jesus isn't about whipping people into shape and making them follow a set of rules. Jesus is about enabling us to experience the fierce grace that shows up in the boot (of grief, loss, or letting go) and that helps us realize that we are clinging tightly to things that maybe don't matter to Jesus.

This is where fun and exciting and potentially heretical and/or reorienting questions come into play. When we ask these questions (and are open to hearing the answers), we can be inspired by the Holy Spirit to create new things that share

Jesus with the marginalized in a more engaging, enriching, and grace-filled way (if Jesus can die and be resurrected, why do we think the church can't be reformed from the ground up?). We must ask hard questions about the status quo. Questions like, What if we allow the unhealthy, hurtful, or unhelpful ways of being together die or burn away? What if we do a hard reboot and completely reorganize our institution in a way that puts first those on the margins? Is this theological box helping or hurting us in our relationship with the world? What would make us more Christ-like? How am I to best emulate God in life? And the inverse (and dreaded) question for many people, myself included, "Am I a hypocrite and how do I stop this?"

Mojo Cookies, Angst, and Prayer

This question of "Am I a hypocrite?" came up in my September 2018 direction session with Mindy. In August we talked about the Apostles' Creed and how I was feeling like the form didn't do justice to the amazingly beautiful God that I know. At the end of the August direction session it became clear that God didn't care about whether people stayed in the box or not, but I still did. September rolled around, and I had finished reading *Insurrection*. The book talks about the radical nature of the crucifixion and the resurrection. It unpacks how we use religion as a psychological crutch to make us feel better about ourselves, our lives, the world, and even God without having to transform our inner nature. I started to wonder if there were ways that I used my idea of God as a psychological crutch.

A few years ago I made these things called "mojo cookies" for my husband as a gesture of my love for him when he was going off to a regional competition for Fly Fishing Team USA. Bad idea for me. Pat is more superstitious than Major League baseball players, and he won the competition with the first batch of mojo cookies if my memory serves. So of course, I have had to make them for every major competition since. Trust me they're nothing special, the recipe is from my Betty Crocker cookbook. The most recent time I made these cookies was the day of his departure for Italy, in September 2018, and I was having an extraordinarily hard time praying for Pat and his teammates. I felt like I was just going through the motions and didn't feel like my prayers were purposeful. The questions "Does prayer even matter?" and "Why am I praying?" popped into my head. I was full of internal angst. Usually I pray for safety, for success, and for well-being. This year I couldn't bring myself to pray for any of that.

However, I felt like Pat expected the mojo cookies to be prayed over for winning and success and all these things that I really don't care about (Pat has enough competitive spirit and desire to win for the both of us), and I didn't want to pray those prayers. I did pray that they experience God in a way that brings them closer in relationship to God, but that wasn't what I felt Pat desired. He doesn't know what I pray, so I'm not sure why this prayer mattered to me... except for the fact that I'm generally concerned with doing the "right" thing and I felt like I wasn't doing it. As I made the cookies, I had this internal wrestling match with myself and eventually gave up as they went into the oven.

I met with Mindy just hours after seeing Pat off at the airport. I told her about my general prayer angst and my concern of using prayer as a psychological crutch, not just for the mojo cookies but also for the prayers that are brought out during prayer time at worship (in small churches). Why are we really praying? What purpose does it serve? Why do we pray for "traveling mercies" (which sounds incredibly odd to me when I'm feeling judgmental)? Does God really care what we pray about, especially if it's trivial or insignificant in the grand scheme of life? Mindy is always entertained by the dramatic swings of my internal pendulum. It gets pretty violent sometimes. Mindy engaged me where I was at: the notion that prayer is B.S.

Hurricane Florence was hammering the Carolinas as we were meeting. We talked about the implications of praying for the hurricane to move paths. If it seemed like God answered the prayer, then why would God move the hurricane's destruction from one place to another? That doesn't seem right. I voiced that it seemed like the only prayer to pray, if we're still talking about Hurricane Florence, is to pray that it doesn't hit land and stays out to sea. But then we discussed that this prayer didn't seem right either, because it could still hurt others if it changes paths. It occurred to me that, in many ways, prayer had become a way for people to control (or think they're controlling) outcomes. It had more to do with prescriptions, expectations, and self-service than it did with anything else. And that didn't seem like prayer to me. It wasn't the kind of prayer in which I wanted to participate.

As Mindy and I continued to unpack prayer and its purpose, I came to the conclusion that if we weren't growing in love in our relationship with God (a.k.a. prayer), then we weren't doing something right, or we weren't positioning ourselves in relation to God in a way that would provide for transformation, which to me is the purpose of the whole thing. I decided (for the moment at least) that prayer is more about showing love for and honoring others, ourselves, the world, and God than it is about specific outcomes and expectations (ahem, control).

Relationship and love, that's what God wants for all of us. And that is what prayer is all about.

My deepest desire was for Pat and his teammates to experience the love of God and participate in that flow, to enjoy the beauty of the Italian Dolomites, and maybe learn something about themselves in the process. The team had a bad third session, and I wasn't looking forward to my husband coming home and being as unpleasant as a wet honey badger. But even so, I couldn't bring myself to pray for a top three finish for each of the Team USA competitors because it just wasn't important to me. However, what was important to me was that they experience God's love and presence during the last day of competition. Before the final two sessions, (sessions four and five), I prayed for them to experience the deep and abiding love of God in a way that connected them to creation (specifically the trout), allowed them to embody God's fierce grace, and connected them to this grace.

This idea of prayer as a means of deepening our relationship with God (and not as a way of controlling outcomes) makes me think of Jesus healing people as he went through various towns. In Luke 17, there's a story of Jesus healing ten lepers. These lepers begged for healing and Jesus told them to go show themselves to the priests. One man noticed that he has been healed while on his way to the priests, and he returned to Jesus to thank and praise God. All ten lepers' prayers were answered, but only a Samaritan man came back (oh the irony!) to give praise where it was due. Jesus' purpose in healing them wasn't so they could be healed. Not completely anyway. Yes, a leper who received healing would be restored to his family and community. This would provide for a new lease on life, bring the healed man back from the margins of society, and allow him to participate fully in the community. However, I think Jesus was more interested in the relationship between the healed and God. Jesus wanted people to be fully restored, in the multiple ways that looked during Jesus' ministry. If we look at many of the healing stories, people who were healed began to follow Jesus around. They went and told their friends and because of this sharing, the crowds around Jesus got bigger. The healed wanted to continue being near Jesus in some way and bring others to know him too.

Heresy World, Hypocrisy, and Self-Reflection

My spiritual journey often feels like the orbit of a comet around the sun: super-elliptical. There are a couple comets, one being Haley's Comet, that come really close to the Sun and then orbit out far from the Sun. Sometimes I feel very near to traditional Christian orthodoxy, and sometimes I feel very far away. Mindy always reminds me that I am in fact orbiting the Sun, even if I perceive that I'm out past Pluto.

My husband tells me I'm weird all the time, and it's usually not a compliment. But I've never been one to live well under the constraints of others' expectations or ideas that don't fit well anymore. I can't even follow a recipe without tinkering with it in some way (including the mojo cookies: I don't add nuts and I use a different amount of chocolate chips than called for in the recipe). An even better example might be when I refused to like Matchbox 20 in college because they were too main-stream, and everyone else liked them. I've generally always distrusted group-think, even when it comes to pop music. Some people see this creativity as brave or adventurous, others find it annoying, and some people find it threatening.

I'm most fascinated by the people who find Heresy World threatening. I wonder what would happen to them if their theological structure was demolished. Would they walk away from the idea of God entirely? Would they lose their sense of identity? What are they holding onto so tightly that is impeding them from experiencing the freedom of fierce grace?

What I've learned from fierce grace is that clutching tightly to things severely limits our ability to grow and transform. When we are unwilling to let things go, we automatically block fierce grace's work in that area (at least for the time being). One of my favorite expressions I use in spiritual direction with people is "Hold things loosely." If we hold our hands in tight fists all the time, we are not able to either let go of what we're clutching or to receive something new. When we hold things loosely, with open hands, we innately give fierce grace permission to take our old ideas and beliefs and replace them with more life-giving options. It's this exchange of one idea for another (or none at all) that increases our freedom, and fierce grace is a major part of this process. I'll continue vacationing in Heresy World as long as fierce grace is giving out tickets because going there is one of the ways I remember to hold my beliefs and ideas about God loosely.

I am on a mission not only to tinker with most things (including religion's signs, symbols, and expressions of faith), but also to make my external and internal worlds as cohesive as possible. My actions and my beliefs had better be in alignment, and when they're not, I want to figure out why. I don't want to be the person whom others look at and say, "Wow, she's a walking contradiction and reflects Jesus poorly." It certainly goes against my Enneagram Type One-ness. Throughout my life, I have experienced the invitation of fierce grace as an invitation to wholeness, integration, and love. Identifying where each one of my beliefs don't align with my actions and then working on aligning them one at a time is a fascinating and fun spiritual discipline to me. I am struck by the transforming power that this process has and leads me to the question: Can we, the church, be brutally honest with ourselves? Are we willing to acknowledge that we are hypocrites and simultaneously embrace and change it so we can reach more people with the abundant love of God?

One of the steps in Alcoholics Anonymous is to take a ruthless self-inventory of one's character. As people of faith (of any kind, not just Christianity), there's this constant invitation to more fully live into who we have been created to be. Living into this potential isn't possible if we are unable to shed our old, ill-fitting, or false behaviors and beliefs. Sometimes we are invited to take this ruthless self-inventory that sheds light in places we don't want to look. Sometimes this inventory leads to an acknowledgment of hypocrisy. Other times it leads to highlighting a lack of self-care. Other times it leads us to make an apology to someone for something we said or did that was unkind. Sometimes, most surprisingly to me, it leads to a "Well done you!" from Jesus. But not that often, like once every five years!

I like to think that John Wesley would have liked AA because one of Wesley's small group questions was "How is it with your soul?" If we're willing to be honest with ourselves, most of the time our souls aren't great. There's something we're struggling with, we can't figure a problem out, we made a bad decision that has impacted our future, etc. Fierce grace invites us to look at, explore, and poke our hypocrisy in a supportive, loving, and accountable environment. Fierce grace vacations with us in Heresy World and enjoys the trip.

For those who might be hesitant to vacation in Heresy World, it's quite possible that they don't know or want to believe that the "Dark Night of the Soul" is a thing. Losing the felt sense of God in a dark night can seem unbearable for many people, and it was for me at first too. Yet it shouldn't surprise us that fierce grace works through the dark night, in a quiet and secret way that leads to radical transformation.

Chapter 9

Attachment, Dark Night, & Hidden Transformation

Sometimes the beginning of a journey can't be understood without first knowing what came later, and I feel like this is how my story of transformation has unfolded. This reasoning is why I'm recounting my first two dramatic experiences of God as an adult here in chapter nine. I would not be who I am without each unique twist and turn along the way, but the very beginning of my transformation has been a lot to internalize and process. I still wonder about much of it. Many odd things happened when I began opening myself up to God. I use the word "odd" intentionally because they were incredibly strange to me and I couldn't explain what was happening with science, but I knew these experiences were real.

In June 2007 I attended a prayer workshop at my church partly out of responsibility but mostly out of a desire to find out what it meant to be in relationship with God. I was on a team focused on increasing my church's passion for spirituality, and there were several members of this team who modeled what it meant to be a mature Christian. They prayed, spent time reading the Bible, and had something I couldn't put my finger on but wanted. By explaining how they listened to God and how they asked for guidance, I started learning what it means to be in a serious relationship with God, and I wanted more. My honesty about my total lack of knowledge and sincere desire to learn about prayer spurred the team to host a prayer workshop that taught about different ways of praying.

It was at this prayer workshop that I encountered Jesus in a very profound way. I didn't audibly hear God's voice, but felt very strongly in my gut that God was asking me to "put up or shut up." I felt Jesus ask me, "are you going to follow me or not?" Along with this question came a surge of energy that I physically felt zoom through my body. It was like I got zapped with electricity. With this newfound energy I was opened up to the possibility that living the way I had been wasn't what God wanted for me, hence the question of whether I was going to follow him. I had no idea what was coming, but I knew my life was going to be very different. Surprisingly I was willing to trust God in this way. It felt like a huge leap for me, and I was scared. At the same time, I knew that if I wanted the best out of life, I needed to follow Jesus and find out what he meant.

One of the last things the workshop leaders did was give away a free registration to the organization's conference on Holy Spirit-filled living in July of that year. It was funny because Daisy, myself, and another friend were sitting in the pews waiting for the winner's name to be called. Before the name was drawn from the basket, Daisy and our friend turned to me and said, "You're going to win the registration." My gut agreed with them, and I was announced as the winner.

Not coincidentally, the organization's conference overlapped another conference I had already committed to. I felt like God was asking me to choose between good and best, that the Holy Spirit-filled living conference was the "best" option for me at the time. After a bunch of internal wrestling, I changed my plans and went to the July 2007 conference on Holy Spirit-filled living—in Arkansas of all places.

The Story of Hot Hands

This conference in Arkansas began with a day of prayer and then had smaller workshops in the afternoon with general assembly-type sessions at night and in the morning. The overall conference attendance was around 1,200 people, and the organizers had provided many different workshops to accommodate the attendees' numbers and differing interests. As I looked through the workshop options, I decided on ones that would help me use my gifts and talents for God. Based on a spiritual gifts inventory I took some time before attending the conference in July 2007, the test indicated I had the gift of faith. But I didn't know what to do with it, which is why I chose a spiritual gifts workshop. I needed something to DO with my spiritual gift, and faith seemed like a fruitcake gift at best. It wasn't useful, at least in my eyes. I listened to the workshop leader break down the nine spiritual gifts in 1 Corinthians into groups of three. The three that he bound together that I thought applied to me were faith, healing, and miracles. I didn't have the latter two and frankly didn't want them. Picture this: a petite, high-strung, perfectionistic and control-freak engineer is stuck to her seat in a workshop on spiritual gifts. Stuck. Like there was an invisible seat belt keeping me in the chair. I couldn't move. I was seriously displeased.

I went back and forth with God, trying to bargain my way out of the room without being prayed for. I sat in the chair until almost everyone had left, and I finally relented because I just wanted out of there. I agreed to be prayed for, although I didn't see the point. I walked up to these two guys and said, "I have the gift of faith, but I don't have the gift of healing or miracles. So, I'm not sure what to do with my gift of faith." They smiled at me and said, "Ok, can we pray for you about this?" I agreed, albeit reluctantly.

Well holy crap on a cracker. I don't know what all they prayed over me, but when they asked God to give me the gifts of healing and miracles my hands felt like they had been electrified. They tingled and got hot and I was afraid to touch anything for half an hour. I'm pretty sure I looked like I had seen a ghost as I ran out of that room and away from those two guys. I don't remember exactly, but I seem to recollect I literally ran away from them. I met my mentor in the hallway as I went back to my room to hide. I told her what happened, and she just smiled at me like she knew something I didn't know, which was completely true. I had no idea what had happened to me, and I was completely freaked out. I got to my room and immediately called Daisy, my prayer partner and soul sister. She still laughs when she thinks about the voicemail I left her, recounting this story. She reminded me recently that in this voicemail I called my hot hands a weird and freakish superpower.

After my initial freak-out, I calmed down a bit and was able to talk to a couple people at the conference about this experience. They helped me understand what these gifts were for and gave me some tips on how and when to use them. Over the next few months as I explored how God wanted to use these gifts through me, I would make comments like, "I think it's time for hot hands." When I prayed for people to be healed, my hands would get hot. It was almost like they were on fire. I got used to this felt sense of God when I prayed for people. Many times I would feel a radiating warmth in my chest as well, kind of like what John Wesley described when he said that his heart was "strangely warmed." I liked that feeling. It was reassuring and let me know that I was doing the right thing and following God's will. It made me think God was with me at those times and that I could trust God.

Be Careful What You Wish For

Over the next couple years I prayed for people as I felt God lead. I learned how to listen to God and felt connected with God in a deep way. Some people were healed, some people were not. Some of the stuff was quite startling; other prayer encounters were very tame. Fierce grace was teaching me about God and how the Holy Spirit operated, and I felt like I was learning in leaps and bounds. But God always seemed to show up in the same way: through my hot hands and warm heart. I had come to expect (ahem, demand?) these signs as God's presence with me. During this time, I discerned a call to professional ministry as a deacon and started seminary in Fall 2008. As I was on a plane to a meeting in Nashville in March 2009, I read an article from a colleague's seminary spiritual direction class about the dark night of the soul. The woman in the article described how she went through this time period where God felt distinctly absent. She got depressed but became a better, more caring, healed, and whole person through the experience. I prayed a dangerous and stupid prayer after I read the article. I prayed that I would go through that experience so I could be a better and more Christ-like person. Dumb. Dumb. Dumb. Dumb. Dumb. Dumb. Dumb. As a general rule, don't ever wish for the dark night. It's not great.

Unfortunately (at the time), my wish was granted that 2009 Advent. I was at an Advent day apart at a local retreat house. I noticed that I had no felt sense of God. None. I rationalized it by thinking that it was because I was praying in a different place and might be distracted since it was the end of the semester. But that was not the case. I continued to feel this significant absence in my spiritual life. I got nothing out of prayer or reading the Bible. There was no inspiration, no insight, nothing. A black void would be a good description. It felt like everything that connected me to God had been severed or sucked away, and I was empty inside.

Even after hoping for a dark night, I didn't realize I was actually in one for four or five months. It's funny how fierce grace works, because in March 2010 I was sitting in a spiritual formation class listening to one of my classmates present on the contemplative stream of spirituality (categorized based on Richard Foster's book *Streams of Living Water*). One person in the group felt led to present on John of the Cross and the dark night, which my professor said was decidedly unusual but worthwhile. As the fellow student described the emptiness, the loneliness, and the dryness that accompanies a dark night, it took everything I had not to burst into tears (and remember, I'm not a crier, especially back then). I realized what was happening. I was in a dark night, and I had asked for it. Stupid, stupid me.

Maybe I have more fight in me than most people who have written about this topic, but nothing I've read about the process or experience of the dark night fully conveys the complete interior reorganization that happened to me. If I were a librarian, it would be like God rearranging all the books in my library every night while I slept. When I entered the library every morning, the books would be in different spots than the day before and there would be book turnover, with some titles leaving and others coming in. I couldn't find what I was looking for, and I spent a ton of time and energy trying to put the books back in an order that I was comfortable with. I was refusing to see that God, through fierce grace, was reordering my internal life in a way that brought more freedom because I was so mad that God kept reorganizing my library. It was exhausting, and after a couple years I finally gave up and let the library be whatever God wanted it to be, although I was still super resentful about the whole thing.

I said before that I got nothing out of prayer during the dark night, but that's not entirely true. After trying all kinds of ways to connect with God and getting the sense that nothing was working, I got mad—seething, fire-breathing dragon mad. When confronted with a similar situation, many other people I've talked to think that it's their fault and start searching all the different ways that their sinful lives could be keeping them from a tangible or felt relationship with God. They stay in this pattern for weeks if not months. Not me. I did a personal sin inventory and within an hour decided that I wasn't the problem (I hope you find this as hilarious as I do). I hurled thirty years of pent up rage, resentment, and hurt at God. God was the problem. God abandoned me. I stayed this way for at least a year, and after that I just got tired and worn out. I didn't have the energy to be physically and emotionally raging against God. It takes a lot of energy to want God to be dead, and that's what I wanted. I was so consumed by the anger that came with my perception of God's abandonment that I wanted to kill God, to stab God in his metaphorical heart. (For those of you who just gasped... Let's be realistic: shit happens. And I'm still here to talk to you so I guess God was okay with it to the point that Jesus and I are tighter than ever.) Even when I wasn't inwardly seething, I was still resentful and bitter. I had a lot of junk to get rid of, which fierce grace worked on in secret while I was pissed at the Trinity. That's pretty nice of her!

Since the felt sense of God had left me and I was tired of being angry, bitter, and resentful, fierce grace prompted me to think that I needed to be okay with this absence by serving God through serving others, kind of like Mother Theresa's experience. At Daisy's prompting, I read Mother Theresa's published letters and was amazed at her purpose and focus in the midst of an uncertain relationship with the Divine. Fierce grace gave me a loving, little shove as I was struck by the love and joy that everyone who encountered her said that she had, even though she didn't recognize or feel it. I find it ironic that the very letters Mother Theresa didn't want to be made public (because she was afraid they would detrimentally impact people's faith) are the very same letters that gave hope to me, Daisy, and many others. Reading about her journey helped me with mine. Through Mother Theresa's writings, fierce grace gave me a different perspective from which to view life. Mother Theresa's experience offered me another option, one that put following Jesus at the center regardless of my potentially bad attitude towards all things Divine.

If I was serious about my Christian journey, I needed to let control go and yield to the process of transformation and trust. My transformation would not, could not be on my terms. Bummer. (I still wrestle with this desire to control my spiritual growth, but I'm getting better at noticing when it happens and more quickly offering it back to God with open hands.) If I didn't feel God within my being ever again, I needed to be okay with that. I had to accept and embrace the fact that the felt sense of God is not actually God. I had created a gigantic golden calf out of the feeling I got through prayer, and it needed to go. God isn't confined to our physical, mental, emotional, or relational limitations, and I was being simultaneously invited and forced to let God out of the box I created. I would find different ways to be with God, and that had to be acceptable to me.

With this decision to accept my spiritual situation, my experience of the dark night shifted primarily from anger to dryness. It also helped that I had gone on a low-dose antidepressant right after Thanksgiving in 2011. (Depression and a dark night don't always go together, but in my case they did.) So I lived in what I affectionately call "The Spiritual Neutral Zone" (any Star Trek fans out there? Heeeyy!). Instead of being a buffer zone between the Romulans and the United Federation of Planets, my spiritual neutral zone was this dry but not too dry spiritual place where nothing was all that energizing. I went through the motions of being a Christian, doing what I thought other people expected me to do. I felt obligated to participate in worship and to attend a conference once or twice per year. While others found scripture, sermons, and Bible study inspirational or energizing, I still felt parched and unfed. Right, wrong, or ridiculous, very few people in my circle besides Daisy had gone through a dark night. It left me feeling isolated and lonely because I felt like I couldn't authentically share my experience with anyone without being misunderstood.

In another twist of irony, I was in seminary and preaching at a little congregation two or three times per month during my dark night and depression, which is what kept me studying the Bible and attending church during this time. The only constant personal spiritual practice I had was spiritual direction once a month and it was a lifeline. Mindy held hope for me when I couldn't. Mindy pointed out how she saw fierce grace transforming me in big and small ways. I had to admit that fierce grace was making me a much kinder and better person, but I wasn't feeling anything substantial while it was happening.

Song Fell Silent

While in seminary, I spent a lot of time in my car. My seminary is about two hours from where I live, and I drove down and back once per week during the average semester. Music has been an integral part of my life since I was in utero, and I've always loved to sing, whether with the radio, in school choir, or the hymns and songs in church. I sang a lot. One of the more interesting things that I noticed during the dark night was that I had no desire to sing. Even when, out of habit, I started singing along with the radio in the car, I would stop singing within a line or two. Song was not coming out of me in any way unless I was leading a hymn at the little congregation where I preached.

There was a span of about three years where I had no song within me, unless I was super excited about something, which didn't happen very often. It turns out fierce grace was working on my unhealthy attachment to song and singing in general. I have a good voice and have sung in choirs (off and on) since I was in elementary school. People have complimented me on my voice for decades, but apart from voice lessons I can't really take any credit. My voice is genetic, I sound almost identical to my mother. When my dad sits between us in church, he gets stereo surround sound whether he likes it or not.

For all the enjoyment I derived from singing, I never had the voice I wanted (this is both a physical and existential issue). I wanted to belt out songs like Aretha Franklin or Christina Aguilera, and I didn't have the voice training to do that. My voice would crack when it got to certain notes. Give me an Italian aria, Vivaldi, or some other classical composer and I could go to town, but contemporary music was another matter. Even if I wanted to be able to sing different songs, by using my God-given voice I received validation, acknowledgment, and praise. Part of my identity was wrapped up in my voice and how I sounded. Pride had attached itself to my singing voice, and God decided that this unhealthy identity needed to be broken and reformed. So I fell silent for a while, not realizing that fierce grace was removing this attachment piece by piece during the dark night. Little by little I got back into singing publicly, mostly during worship with a song that went with the message I was giving that day. But these times were few and far between, perhaps once or twice a year. I was always really nervous that I was going to sound bad or make a mistake. I was still concerned about making a good impression and having people think I was competent and talented. I still couldn't honor my voice without pride raising its ugly head.

Throughout the dark night and the spiritual neutral zone, I let singing go and didn't think much of it at the time. I occasionally wondered where the joy went and assumed that the lack of desire to sing was just another part of the dark night. If it came back, then great. If not, that would be fine too. I didn't know that fierce grace was transforming my relationship with my voice during this period. It wasn't something I talked about with anyone, not even my spiritual director, because I didn't think it was consequential. That is, until July 2017.

I went to a Diakonia World Federation conference in July 2017. One of the options given to participants was to play an instrument or sing for our collective times of worship. I volunteered to sing in the choir, since I had liked choir singing before 2009 and there was no commitment past the conference time (the no commitment thing was key!). I expected to feel the same sense of accomplishment, satisfaction, and value as I did pre-2009. But I felt nothing. I was detached.

At the conference, I was conned into singing a verse at an evening prayer gathering by someone in the choir who said she wasn't feeling well. From singing this short verse from "There Is a Balm In Gilead" (not a fan of this song, so it adds to the irony) at a prayer service early during the conference, I got on the choir director's radar. Uh Oh. She asked me to sing a solo at our Fourth of July concert and although everything in my body was screaming "NO!", my mouth said, "Yes, I can do that." The choir director has an uncanny superpower of having people say yes even when they don't want to. I was terrified, or thought I'd be terrified. I hadn't sung in front of that many people (300-400 people) in a long time, and I was really nervous I'd botch the whole thing. During our practice in a neo-gothic cathedral at a Jesuit university with stunning acoustics, I was concerned I wouldn't be heard, so I sung my solo forcefully over the pipe organ. At the end, my voice echoed for two seconds after I had stopped singing. It was kind of like an out of body experience since I had always disliked hearing myself sing. I was so surprised at the clarity and tone of my voice, even in the echo. The concert went off without a hitch, and I sang my solo well.

Throughout the conference's choir rehearsals and singing during worship, I noticed that I didn't get the same feeling from singing that I had in the past. There wasn't a sense of satisfaction, pride, or an undercurrent of superiority. My sense of identity was no longer attached to how well I performed or how many solos I sang. To the contrary, there was a distinct sense of freedom that I wanted to explore more deeply.

Upon returning from the conference, I brought these things to Bill for spiritual direction supervision. There was so much more tied up in music and singing for me than I had ever imagined. During my session with Bill, fierce grace helped identify what had transformed over the last eight years and the impact this transformation had on my well-being. Bill remarked that the freedom I was experiencing had come from the deep purification and cleansing from the dark night. Although he didn't mention fierce grace, I now realize that through Bill's words fierce grace was pointing out how she had been persistently working on this issue in secret, like it was a great surprise. He noted that my true self was able to be present and expressed not only through music and song but also through conversation and speaking. We talked about how there was an interior freedom because the motivation to sing or speak up wasn't from a desire to be recognized but from an innermost truthfulness that was ready to be shared. This shift from desiring recognition to singing as my true self explained why people's compliments at the conference didn't impact my self-worth. Yes, people's comments were reassuring but they didn't prop up my ego like they used to do. They weren't important to my being or true self. It hadn't occurred to me that fierce grace had been at work in this way, yet the fruit was on full display.

A month later I was still pondering this dramatic shift in my relationship to music and song since fierce grace allowed additional insights to bubble up after my session with Bill. In August 2017 Mindy and I talked about these feelings in spiritual direction (she takes July off every year for self-care, we could all learn something from her!). She asked me about what singing used to be like, why I liked singing in a group, etc. Through her questioning I realized that singing in special choirs, whether in college or in a small ensemble community choir after graduation, was a joy. It forced me to be present in the moment, we created something bigger than ourselves, we created beauty, and we connected to people throughout the history of music. But pride and self-worth were also tied up very tightly in my participation in these more elite choirs. I was reminded that singing was a way of praying for me, and since all my other prayer forms disintegrated during the dark night, singing had to disintegrate and be reformed too.

When the desire to sing came back, I mistakenly thought it would be the same as before, and it was decidedly not. I was expecting the same feelings of joy and connection through an exterior locus. Rather, my joy and worth now come from a place deep within. In talking to Jesus about this, he noted that singing is another way I can learn to trust myself (again with the trust issues). Jesus was offering even more interior freedom, a place of healing and rest, and a same but different way to experience prayer.

It's Done, For Now

This transformative same-but-different experience of singing is representative of many other practices in my life. Because of the dark night, prayer has taken on a different meaning and purpose, my participation in church has a changed flavor to it, and my ministry feels like it has exponentially more space than before. If I hadn't gone through the dark night, I would not have been able to shed (as quickly, albeit violently) the negative self-talk, the desperate need for affirmation, or the ego's dominance in my being. The false self would have continued building a thicker and thicker shell, thus burying my true self under layers and layers of self-important activities and accolades. Something had to give, and I broke wide open.

As Daisy and I talked recently about this period in our lives, we ended up giggling quite frequently at how our idiocy, pride, self-importance, and image mattered so much to us ten years ago. We both agreed it was like these things were steam-rolled out of us, with the steam roller catching us continually by surprise. It took all the energy we had to just pull ourselves out of bed every morning to be confronted with more character issues that needed to go from our beings. Although we didn't feel bad for people at the time (giggle giggle), we now have some deep compassion for those who lived with us or were around us during the really dark times of 2010-2011. It couldn't have been very pleasant living with us.

But even as much as I pseudo-lament over the soul-crushing angst and turmoil of those years, I wouldn't change my process of transformation for anything or anyone. I am so grateful that God's unconditional grace and love focused itself so mercilessly on my character and being. One of my mottos still is "Go big or go home." If you're going to do something, do it well, make it have a big impact, or don't do it at all. God showed up to me in a way that I really couldn't miss. God went big, hitting me over the head with a two by four, wearing me down until I didn't have an ounce of fight left in me (for that moment anyway). I wouldn't be the person I am today without those years of intense culling and reorientation. I am unreservedly grateful for this experience. Even though I was walking out of the dark night, fierce grace wasn't finished showing me ways I had gotten attached to other false god-images.

Chapter 10

Protection & Abandonment

After beginning to come out of the dark night in late 2017, I thought that almost everything about my life had been reoriented. The fight in me was still there but had been purified substantially. Old behavior and thought patterns were leaving for good (for the most part), and I had developed a healthy sense of self that relies on who I am in Christ and not what I do or how I do it. However, even this dramatic transformation didn't stop me from creating unhealthy attachments to god-images. I somehow developed this idea that God was my protector against all odds and regardless of the situation.

God, Where Are You?

For the last couple years, I have seen Jesus as my big brother, someone to guide me but also to protect me and the ones I love. My desire to be protected was worked out in my own life through trying to protect myself and others. I didn't realize the full effect of this until this year when I noticed that I have a defensive and habitual pattern of wanting to protect people, places, and things, regardless of whether it's my responsibility to protect in that way. My desire for a protecting God was projected onto other people and things as objects to guard. It's fascinating to me how these things work. One of my fears is abandonment, specifically by the people (or God) in whom I've invested myself deeply and with whom I have significant relationships. Projecting an image of a defending God onto Jesus was one of the ways that I was keeping myself safe from emotional pain and abandonment. If God was my protector, then I couldn't be abandoned.

This understanding of a protecting Jesus crept in so subtly over the last couple years that I didn't realize it had become unhealthy, an idol even. I mistakenly expected Jesus to protect me, the ones I love, and our possessions without exception and at all costs. This unspoken expectation was one of the reasons I was so upset with God when Shaquille died. Jesus should have protected her from disease while she was in the prime of life. My head knew that this was not how God works, but my heart really wanted it to be so.

As 2017 rolled into 2018, I was having a hard time listening to men tell me how to live my spiritual life. I didn't want any man, even Jesus, to dictate how I should live my life as a faithful and embodied woman created in the image of God. Men just didn't get it. Then Shaq the wonder-bunny died. With this emotional schism, my faith and trust in God decreased significantly. I felt deeply wounded by Jesus' abandonment of me and my little girl. I apparently had some deep-seated expectations of which I was unaware. Jesus should have protected her. Jesus was supposed to take care of those people I loved, and that meant that they wouldn't die unexpectedly, especially Shaquille. In my bitter disappointment with God, fierce grace took it upon herself to get my attention. She wanted to help me uncover this unrealistic expectation and was willing to use any means necessary to do it. Fierce grace chose to poke and prod me through my dreams.

The unraveling of my hurt and disappointment started with a dream from fierce grace. It was a very vivid dream and I remembered most of it when I wrote it in my journal. I generally don't remember my dreams, and having it seem as real as watching a movie got my attention. What follows is the summary of the dream.

A woman who owns a farm invited me to housesit for her while she was away. I agreed and flew across the US, arriving at the airport, getting a taxi to take me to the farm. I arrived, stumbled up the porch steps with all my baggage, and entered the kitchen. Leaving my luggage by the door, I wandered around the farm, exploring the grounds and farmhouse that felt quite cluttered. There was extra furniture, stacks of books, and miscellaneous items all over the house. As I was exploring the basement, I heard someone come in the kitchen door and bump into my bags. I hurried upstairs ready to fight, and this twenty-something man was standing in the doorway looking quizzically at the large amount of luggage I brought with me. After brief introductions, I find out that he's a farmhand and stays at the house. My friend didn't tell me about any farmhand so I was skeptical. I went to take one of my suitcases upstairs and get settled. When I returned, this farmhand had made himself quite comfortable sitting on the couch with his feet on the coffee table, watching TV with a sandwich and soda in the living room. I quipped, "You seem to have made yourself right at home, haven't you?" He laughed and said, "Why yes I have, considering this is my home. Your friend is my mother, and I live here." Heat rose to my face, and I stomped out of the room, going to find a way to confirm this guy's story with my friend. Unfortunately for me the phone was broken, and the internet didn't work. So I gave up, and we both stayed at the farmhouse, which was the end of the dream.

In the dream, this farmhand made me incredibly uncomfortable for several reasons; but there are two that struck me that I pondered for days afterwards. The first was that he was completely happy with who he was. He wasn't trying to impress anyone, and he fit in his skin and enjoyed being human in a way I had not experienced. It was panic-inducing because I couldn't fathom such an existence. Who would I be if I wasn't trying to be the best and do the right thing all the time? As I prayed with the ideas and images from the dream, I brought the image of the farmhand to mind. As I went through this mental process in prayer, it occurred to me that the farmhand was inviting me to experience life in the same way he did, to receive the gift that is life and love from the divine creator. I experienced this invitation silently, just by making eye contact with the farmhand in my imaginative prayer time. It was electrifying in a way, but also gave me a strong desire to run and hide in a closet without actually being able to do so. The second thing that took me by surprise as I prayed with the image of the farmhand and the farmhouse was that it felt like he could see right through all of my defenses within two seconds of walking in the house. My carefully curated façade didn't work with him. Bummer. I hadn't felt that vulnerable in a long time, and I wasn't happy that this farmhand could see right through me. I became stuck, literally and figuratively in an awkward dance with this farmhand as we stayed at the house together during my prayer times. Yet I refused to give up talking with the farmhand in prayer because I knew fierce grace was inviting me to dig deeper and get to the root of still-unnamed issues hindering my relationship with God.

It was deeply unsettling for me to be invited to be loved by God out of gift and generosity, not from earning or production. I didn't like the invitation one bit, so I brought this dream and my prayer times to my spiritual ninja, Mindy. Mindy loves working with dreams in our direction sessions, usually much to my dismay and increased internal freedom. While I was telling her the dream, it occurred to both of us that Wisdom (more on Wisdom in the next chapter) was the woman who owned the farm and Jesus was the farmhand. The more I reimagined this dream in our direction session, the more anxious I became. I was increasingly resistant to the invitation to be loved for who I am, to receive grace from Farmhand Jesus or anyone else. I needed more time. I wasn't ready to experience this kind of fierce grace just yet. Mindy understood, and noted that it was quite possible that the excessive amount of luggage I brought with me was representative of many things I was carrying around that maybe I didn't need anymore, and it would take time to unpack all that was held within. Just maybe fierce grace was inviting me to unpack the baggage with Jesus. Maybe. We ended our session with me agreeing to spend more time with Farmhand Jesus in prayer, learning to relax and be comfortable in my own skin while unpacking the suitcases to see what didn't fit anymore. From our direction session I realized that this dream had several layers that weren't going to be resolved in one meeting. Fierce grace had a lot to share, and it was going to take a while. I braced myself for impact and kept pondering this dream and its ramifications.

Over the next three weeks or so, I had conversations during my prayer time with Farmhand Jesus, Wisdom, and the luggage I brought upstairs into the guest bedroom. I admit it sounds strange to have a conversation with a suitcase, but if Jungian dream theory is correct that everything in the dream is a part of me, then the suitcase is a part of my being and wanted to give some input. At fierce grace's nudge, Suitcase and I had a prayerful conversation. I learned that I wasn't done protecting my heart from the world.

After some tough negotiations with Suitcase at the beginning of my prayer time, She let me open her up, and inside I found clothes surrounding two sea green glass orbs. The larger orb, according to Suitcase, was my heart. Suitcase was carrying around my heart. She believed that because I've had a lot of disappointment and loss in my life, my heart needed to hide to stay safe. Guarding it was her responsibility, and she took great pride in having my heart packed tightly away and well hidden. I responded to Suitcase, "What if I told you that isn't my heart anymore?" Suitcase didn't understand, so I told her "That's an old heart. A heart that had hardened and became very brittle. My heart now is full of love and is soft and malleable. You can't break that which is resilient. That's not my heart. It's beautiful but not mine anymore." Suitcase was perplexed and somewhat let down. She said, "But I've been carrying it around and protecting it for you. For. So. Long." I responded by thanking her for her effort, thanking her for her commitment and desire to keep me from being hurt. But I also reinforced that the glass orb wasn't me anymore. I asked Suitcase if we could hang up the orb in a place it could catch the light and sparkle, and she agreed as long as Heart was okay with it. We hung up the orb in the window, and it cast beautiful shadows of brilliant seafoam green around the room. One layer was peeled back, but there were so many more to go...

As I continued to sit in imaginative prayer with Farmhand Jesus and Suitcase and her contents, more and more resistance bubbled up, especially from Heart. Heart refused to talk to me or Jesus, so at fierce grace's suggestion I invited Wisdom to come sit with us and take over the conversation. Maybe Wisdom could make a breakthrough that Jesus and I couldn't. Heart and Wisdom had a verbal sparring match, which was quite interesting to watch. Heart said she was fine, F.I.N.E. fine.

Wisdom, in her loving sassiness responded, "You know what that stands for right? F-ed up, insecure, neurotic, and emotional. You really want to be fine?" I like that Wisdom isn't afraid to bring the thunder. Heart fought back, calling Jesus surly, fickle, and a liar. Wisdom in her great and fierce grace asked, "So what Jesus promises in the Bible are lies?" Heart, replied without skipping a beat (sorry, not sorry for the bad pun), "Yes. Or we've interpreted them so incorrectly that it seems that way. At face value, yes, Jesus lies, at least in terms of my expectations. He's supposed to take care of us, to protect us, to guide us. And yet this world is so messed up. And Shaq died because of my relationship with Jesus. She was taken because of us."

Yowsers. Up until this point (almost four months after Shaquille died), I didn't realize how much I blamed myself for her death. I was bearing the full responsibility while simultaneously resenting Jesus because he didn't protect her. Heart continued, "I feel like we can't get ahead or catch a break." Wisdom asked, "So Jesus is supposed to help with that?" "Yes," Heart hesitantly responded. After a pause she continued, "But maybe not. Maybe he just stands with us through the pain." Immediately I ruptured, and tears streamed down my face. I broke open again in a way that let hidden beliefs out into the light. I was caught up in the lie that Jesus should protect me and the people I love from everything and that my life should go smoothly as a Christian. Fierce grace reminded me that Jesus promises to be with us and experience what I experience, not to fix things to make our lives comfortable or pain-free.

With this conversation between Heart and Wisdom, fierce grace helped me acknowledge an idol and then let it die. In this death I saw everything new again. A great ideological and theological burden was left behind because fierce grace was persistent in getting my attention. I felt such a sense of interior freedom, like a heavy weight had been lifted from my heart. My body, mind, and heart felt so much lighter, like the emotional burden of believing in the false god-image had sunk into my bones and weighed me down without me knowing. Jesus doesn't need to be my protector AND he didn't abandon me. Revelatory. Seriously.

Lesson learned: when in doubt (or when tired of the tension, emotional exhaustion, etc.), maybe consider inviting Wisdom into the conversation.

Another False God-Image Gone

This experience of fierce grace through dream work and imaginative prayer was a catalyst for another dramatic reorientation of my whole being, for which I am grateful. In talking to my husband about my demeanor, he remarked that he never knows who to expect because I am a different person every six to eight months. I asked him if it was a better person and he said "Generally, yes." That was one of the best compliments anyone could ever give me. And in 2018 my rate of noticeable transformation quickened to every three months in the first half. People who hadn't seen me for a few months remarked in April that I had a distinctly different demeanor, one that was much calmer and peaceful, more grounded and less frantic. I thanked them for noticing while thinking, "Yeah, that's because I got the shit beat out of me over the last three months and had my 'rightness and control' toy broken against my will." Then there was the next shift at the end of May, and the next in September, and the next invitation in October and then November. I refuse to be stagnant in my faith, which leads to a rather large amount of transformation. I am a different person fairly regularly, and that's a good thing.

Even with all the things that happened in 2018, I still have the desire to protect people from suffering. I'm still in process of letting go. This desire to be protected and to protect others is so ingrained that it's going to take some time to dissipate. One difference that I'm noticing is that I'm okay with the process of acknowledging the desire to protect (that would cross healthy boundaries) and not acting on it, which is one of the ways fierce grace is encouraging me to grow right now.

I Am Enough, Again

Fierce grace is still reminding me that presence, my presence, is enough. I don't have to strive or make things difficult or try to protect people. Those things take a ton of energy away from actually living into wholeness. I highly value efficiency, and wasting energy trying to guard people from suffering or preventing hardship is the opposite of efficient. It separates me from myself, it puts my mind, heart, and body at odds with one another when they're supposed to be working together. I want to live in harmony with myself, the Trinity, and Wisdom.

Harmony requires presence, listening to one another to sing or play together in both unison and unity while singing different notes that weave in and through each other. Singing in unison, where the group sings the same notes together, can be powerful, but singing with a group in harmony brings a sense of depth, connectedness, and wonder to the magical world of music and song. In our unique voices and parts, we combine to create something so much bigger and more beautiful than each of us individually could imagine. And if I'm going to participate fully with fierce grace in the harmony, I must think of myself as enough. I must believe with every cell and particle in my body that the sound coming out of my mouth, and the beauty being created from me and with me is enough. I must experience joy in the present moment of harmony. If I bring all of who I am to the journey, being present with heart, mind, and body without trying to protect anyone or anything, it is enough.

Chapter 11

Invitation to Dance

In January 2018 I was having a really hard time listening to any man tell me how to live my life or live out my spirituality, including Jesus. He didn't have a say either. Naturally, I was in direction with Mindy talking about this issue. She asked me questions about my resistance to male figures and suggested that I ask God for an image or female person with whom I could relate better. We took a few minutes of silence, and all of a sudden this woman showed up as a vision in my mind. Like a movie being projected on the interior of my eyelids, "She" showed up. It took me a few weeks to realize her name is Wisdom. She appeared to be of Native American descent and was dressed in gray and white tie-dye flowing garments with a thick belt, which matched her long, coarse, wavy, gray and white hair. She was dancing around a fire pit somewhere in the desert of the Southwest US. I was struck by her presence, joy, and beauty.

Since this was the image I received, I mentally vented in her general direction about how dumb it was to create male and female and the duality that was inherently born out of the two, etc., etc. She didn't care what I thought, which was very strange to me. Instead of arguing, She sat and listened to my tantrum with a smile on her face and a twinkle in her eye. When I told this to Mindy, she asked if She was God. With this question I realized that I have wanted a strong and protective God, and I attributed those characteristics to a masculine god. Mindy reminded me that in most of nature the protector parent is actually the female, that it is the mother who is fiercely protective. Hmm. Animals like bears, falcons, and whales are all fierce in protection of their young. The words "fierce grace" came to mind as I reflected on her. She, this new god-image, is fierce without being aggressive, domineering, or controlling. She was inviting me to be all the things I tried to be in my twenties but came across as a rigid and unrelenting bulldozer because I was deathly afraid of failure.

As I sat with She in imaginative prayer after my January direction session, I tried to have conversations with her, but She chose not to speak for some reason. She was so unusual to me and had a vast freedom that I envied. She was perfectly content in her body. As I prayerfully pictured the fire pit where we met, I watched She revel in the movement of her body around the fire. She was totally unconcerned with what I thought of her and my staring in amazement. Her flowing skirt and sleeves moved like flags in the wind and her long gray and white hair whipped around her when she twirled with glee. I was transfixed by her joy and her "I don't care what you think of me" attitude that was deeply rooted in love. During these imaginative prayer times, I sat in silence and watched her dance, unsure of who She actually was and why she showed up. More importantly, She wanted me to join her in the dance, and I refused.

As I sat with her in prayer through February and March, I realized She was Wisdom and started calling her by name. The more I learned about her, the more I related to her, the more I wanted to be in conversation with her. I was open enough that she took up residence in me. It felt like Wisdom was living in the space where the Holy Spirit resides, that deep part of my gut that is both physically real and unreal at the same time. I wanted Wisdom to be there, to guide me, to educate me, and to be present with me even if she wasn't responding to me with words just yet. It was interesting to me that Wisdom chose not to speak to me at first, probably because I wasn't ready to hear what she had to say (that whole pearls before swine thing... and I was the swine in this situation!). It took me a while after Shaq's death to be open enough to hear what Wisdom might share, and I think my heart was also afraid of her freedom. She was a lot to take in, so different from the way I experienced myself and the world.

Refusing Fierce Grace

In general I have a hard time letting things go, especially if I can't control the outcome. I received an Enneagram Type One email just this morning that encouraged me to stop obsessing about things over which I have no control...which is funny. It's a pattern. These things happen. I needed the reminder. The other factor in this personality trait of obsessing over things is that I like to make sure I finish the job. Everything must be complete before I move on to the next thing, at least in terms of my spiritual life.

As mentioned in the last chapter, 2018 was filled with fierce grace prodding me with vivid dreams to remember and write down. I had dreams where I'm traveling, giving other people's stuff back to them, house-sitting, and taking things apart or leaving things behind. There's been a distinct theme of fierce grace throughout the dreams, encouraging me to give up emotional or spiritual stuff that isn't mine or doesn't fit anymore and to embrace what Trinity has prepared for me, even if I'm not done with the old stuff yet. In every single dream there has been some issue with me leaving the old behind to be cleaned up by someone else. Whether I run back to collect my luggage when others are inviting me to let it go or I'm so focused on a demolition project that I don't see what God has already built for me, my psyche was having a hard time embracing the fierce grace of letting things go.

During the summer of 2018 I brought two distinct yet related dreams to share with my small group. Both dreams were about me being unwilling to embrace something new, and both dreams included the Trinity wanting to give me a gift that they had prepared especially for me. In these dreams I refused the gifts from the Trinity and wanted to go back to the project I was working on because it wasn't finished yet. I had an unhealthy obsession with finishing what I started, even in my dreams, and didn't feel like I could accept Trinity's gifts without completing the previous project. As my small group discussed these two dreams, I was asked "What is it about the gift that makes you unable to receive it?" I responded, "I didn't earn it or do anything to deserve it." We all sat in expectant quiet for a moment before I said, "That's the definition of grace, isn't it? <starting to laugh> Why on earth can I help other people accept it but have such a hard time welcoming it in my own life?" Everyone laughed along with me because this issue is universal. We think we don't deserve God's love and grace, being invited to the dance, or however it shows up. We think we have to do "enough" to be worthy of love. And yet. God's fierce grace continues to offer itself to us, hoping that eventually we'll receive the gift.

As I've gone through this year of grief and tremendous personal transformation, Wisdom has been constantly inviting me to dance with fierce grace, and I've refused. And I've refused for lots of reasons, but I think primarily out of the desire to control situations and outcomes. I didn't want to dance because

I had other things to work on, things that I could control, or so I thought. As is usual for spiritual direction, Mindy and I were having a conversation about my spiritual life, and I mentioned a dream for us to talk about. In the dream I visited Wisdom's farmhouse again, and the Trinity (Creator, Jesus, and Holy Spirit) was there sitting on the porch watching me take down a derelict, detached garage. They must have gotten tired of watching me do demolition because Jesus came over and invited me to get on a tractor to see something new. He took me to see a three or four-story, new, red and shiny round barn. Trinity had built this round barn for me, it was their gift to me. Yet when I woke up and sat with the dream, I was fixated on getting back to the garage to continue to dismantle it. I couldn't let the old garage go without completing the task myself.

As Mindy and I continued our discussion, she encouraged me to imagine Trinity and Wisdom and what they might be inviting me to do. As I sat in silence with my eyes closed, I received a vision of a fire pit in the desert, similar but not exactly like the one Wisdom had been dancing around for months. A fire was burning, with the edge of the fire pit demarcated by brick-sized rocks. Then there was a sandy area where Trinity and I were standing in a circle around the fire. A few yards out from the fire was another circle of rock that enclosed the fire pit and standing area. These rocks in the largest concentric circle were big boulders that people could sit on, or as Wisdom was doing, dancing on them in complete joy. Trinity and I were holding hands and moving around the circle in a really simple dance. I was following their lead, wanting them to direct the dance. Then something switched, and they telepathically told me it was time for me to lead the dance. In this prayer vision I stopped short and had some clarifying questions and statements for them, such as "You want me to lead the dance?" "Are you sure this is a good idea?" "I don't want to lead the dance." They stood there around the fire, waiting expectantly for me to start moving. Wisdom was standing on a boulder swaying back and forth, also waiting for me to choose.

After a quick bit of contemplation, I recognized that these four could and would wait me out. They wanted me to dance, whether it was immediately or in two weeks or two months. Fierce grace told me they were going to wait until I said yes. I decided that it couldn't hurt to try and I might as well get this over with. In my prayer vision I started doing these crazy moves that looked similar to the *Seinfeld* episode when Elaine dances at her office party combined with Sandra Bullock's character, Margaret Tate, in the movie *The Proposal* when she dances around a fire pit with Gammy. I started to giggle as Trinity started moving in time with me. They shifted and moved as if we were one being, connected so deeply that no words needed to be said to change the rhythm or step of the dance. Wisdom continued to dance to her own beat on the rocks around us. It was like Wisdom was the thing that hemmed everything in, she made the dance possible. As long as I was dancing with the Trinity within the scope or bounds of Wisdom, all was well. And though the circles in my prayer vision were fairly small, I know that Wisdom is flexible, expansive, encompassing, and permeable. The boulders didn't signify a firm boundary for all eternity. They signified the boundary for which I needed to feel safe at the time. Even now as I picture this dancing place and the rock boundaries, I notice that the circle has already expanded and is almost pulsing with divine energy, like it's alive and vibrant and ready for the adventure.

Results

If you haven't already gathered, I am a results-driven person. I like to see things come into being and then finish well, regardless of what it is. I wouldn't have stayed on this spiritual journey if I hadn't seen distinct and dramatic results of personal transformation. And by hanging out with Wisdom this year, I'm amazed at the world of difference between me in January and me in December. (Although a few nights ago, I had another dream about me being invited to be cared for by others instead of trying to do everything myself, so apparently fierce grace isn't finished with me yet.) I feel like I've been shot out of a cannon every day, multiple times a day, for the last six months. Just when I think I've come to a new spiritual equilibrium, I go flying through the air again without any idea of where I'll land. There's been no relief, no resting on my laurels, no time to catch my breath. For a fleeting moment I might think, "Holy crap on a cracker, is this ever going to slow down?" But then I admit that the deepest part of me is looking at Trinity and Wisdom and saying "Bring it. If this is what life is about, then bring it on." I invite this swift and destabilizing movement of grace. I am intentionally inviting fierce grace to shake up everything about me, and it's made me a more calm, kind, and even-tempered person in the process.

Leaning In To Wisdom

In my November 2018 session with Mindy, we ended up talking about how I thought Jesus' ministry years sucked. Like, they were a terrible time, plodding, a slog, painful. Therefore, if Jesus' time was hard work, then being a Christian had to be hard work too. It couldn't be easy, that would be impossible. Hmm. Maybe not? Mindy and I returned to the red barn's significance, pondering that Trinity had prepared it for me as a gift that I was reluctant to accept. My first instinct was to use the barn as a place to help people, to be a safe place where people could come to bask in Wisdom's presence. During the prayer time I sensed that Wisdom wasn't okay with this idea because it focused on other people. Trinity didn't build the barn for other people, they built it for me, for my own personal enjoyment, for my own respite and a place to put my treasures.

I have a hard time keeping things that are meant solely for me to myself because I don't think I deserve them or I think that they should be shared. Wisdom was encouraging me to put what I loved in the barn, to make it a safe space for myself, to create or curate a place for me that was my sanctuary and a reminder of the journey. Even now, a month later, I'm still having a hard time accepting this gift of specifically reserved and private space. But I also know that tomorrow a switch could flip and I could be completely content with having this beautiful and efficient space for my own interior being. While I was in Ireland right after my session with Mindy, I painted a mug that will be symbolic of the journey. I put it in my office to remind me to bloom and grow. It will be just for me and no one else. It is a marker on my journey, a reminder of a time and place when I was on pilgrimage allowing fierce grace to teach me how to let my journey be easy, like Jesus' yoke.

And I think that the invitation of learning to dance is intricately tied into my ability to believe that Jesus' journey wasn't a slog but a primarily joyful walk with some crap along the way. Wisdom told me (in our conversation during direction with Mindy in November) that Jesus was like a kid in a candy store. He was so excited to see people soften and change from being loved unconditionally that the difficult times were far surpassed by the joy he experienced from being part of the beautiful mess that is creation.

I hadn't thought of it this way, or more likely I didn't believe that this was realistic. I rejected the idea that life could be more joyful and less strenuous. I have been proven wrong. Completely and totally wrong. This makes me smile because I'm glad I was wrong—a hard thing for someone like me to admit with joy. I'm glad that there are other ways to live life than feeling like I have to will things into existence or feeling like everything will take such a significant amount of work that I have to emotionally prepare myself. Going into projects and life in general with the idea that joy can be my first option is radically different than how I've lived my life to this point. I'm excited that I can choose to perceive life as breezy, like I'm not weighed down by concrete shoes or have to give more of myself than I want to in order to make a project or event happen. I'm looking at life like it's a joy instead of a slog. A dance instead of a death march. Hallelujah.

One of the many things I'm learning and finding great joy in is that Wisdom (like fierce grace) shows up in unexpected places. She connects things, creates bridges, and spans differences that seem insurmountable. She is paradox in its purest sense. I'm starting to love paradox. I've liked tension for a while, but I'm starting to love it. It makes me take notice and evaluate whether I'm on the right track. Several years ago, when my pastor encouraged me to "embrace the ambiguity," I had a distinct desire to punch him in the arm. Things needed to be black or white with no gray; I needed the world to be either/or. Little by little, my rejection of and frustration with my pastor's comment has shifted to deep gratitude. With Mindy's help, I've also embraced that things are more often both/and instead of either/or. Paradox, tension, both/and, or whatever you want to call it is the world we live in. Thanks to my pastor, I've shared his words with many other people as I've led groups in Bible study or training and worked with people in spiritual direction.

Humans have this compulsion for certainty, and I've learned that Wisdom and the Trinity just don't care about this issue. They send fierce grace to stir the pot and get us to relinquish our desire to control and have certainty. Ambiguity is good because it keeps us off balance enough to lean into Wisdom and fierce grace and keep them as constant companions.

Finally, I am willing to dance nine months after Wisdom first showed up. As I ponder and reflect on my slow willingness to dance, I recognize that dance is a perfect embodiment of fierce grace for me. I've loved to move and dance since I was little. I switched to tap and jazz in first grade because I thought beginning ballet (in kindergarten) was entirely too boring. I wanted to leap and twirl and jump and fly through the air. But no, we galloped around the room in a circle. Blah! I liked jazz, and we competed as elementary school students, which was great fun. But my first love was tap. There is something magical about body movement and rhythm that makes coordinating sound with the others in the class (It's similar to harmony in a choir).

Even after an almost thirty-year hiatus, there is still something magical and enchanting and badass about tap. Thanks to *The Artist's Way* by Julia Cameron, I started taking tap again this summer. I still love it and am surprised that I still love it. My intermediate adult tap class just performed in the December recital, and we had such a good time. Our steps were clean, we had fun, and we made the audience laugh. Trifecta!

When I'm focused on the steps and movement, it's almost a unitive moment for me. It's me and the music and I feel deeply connected without being body-conscious or worried about whether I look okay in the costume. Fierce grace is inviting me to dance with Wisdom and Trinity in the same way. I can experience the Divine in a unitive flow that is reciprocal. I give of myself, Trinity gives of themselves, I receive, Trinity receives. In Wisdom's dance I am enough. This is what Wisdom has been inviting me to this whole time. She's been inviting me to participate in this unitive dance with the Divine so I can experience and receive fierce grace. It's a dance that ebbs and flows, changes and shifts, recedes and swells just like grief, love, and loss. It's one way of imagining the journey. It's a way of being excited about life, asking myself "How do I get to dance with Trinity and Wisdom today?" "How do I get to experience the flow that is of and from the Divine?" The mystic in me jumps for joy at the possibility of dancing with God every day, having this kind of lovely connection because of fierce grace. This dance flow is something I can "tap" into whenever and as much as I want. I don't have to wait for Wisdom's invitation to dance, it's a standing reservation that offers joy, freedom, abundant life, and enough-ness. Understanding Wisdom's invitation with this framework brings joy to the day instead of expecting a slog.

Joy and gratitude are kind of the point of the journey I think. I work seasonally at a candy store and there was this man who came into the store during Advent who was super stoked about the options we provided him. He was excited about the chocolate-covered cashews and the fact that we gift wrapped the box for him—intensely excited. Most of us who work there don't get that excited about anything, and we're all pretty chill generally speaking. After he left, the assistant manager and I were talking about his attitude. We were amazed he was that genuinely happy. We also laughed that he had no idea how he had made our day better by having what seemed to be such an over the top attitude of joy and gratitude. We don't see that very often in retail. Usually people are complaining about something, but not him, Mr. 982 (he bought $9.82 worth of chocolate-covered cashews. It's an unoriginal name but very specific!). This dude, 982, reminded me very pointedly that I have a choice in my attitude, and I want to choose gratitude and joy.

For me, being present with gratitude leads me to experience divine love that rises from within and radiates out of my being. And even as I revel in the love that I feel from Trinity in this moment, I also realize that my grief is not done. Joy doesn't negate sorrow. Happiness can be fleeting. But it is how we choose to approach life that is what is most important. Am I going to look at life as a plodding and tortuous disaster or am I going to look at it like it's a joyful dance with some missteps along the way? I have a choice. We all have the ability to choose to be like 982.

One of my favorite quotes is from Paula D'Arcy: "God comes to you disguised as your life." If this is in fact the truth (which I firmly believe it is), then everything that comes to us, good or bad, can be an invitation to reach out to the Divine and explore how God is in each breath of our lives. I'm not saying that God causes all things to happen, but I am saying that God is with us through all things. Because God is with me at all times and in all things, I can dance with Trinity and Wisdom whenever I want, provided I remember that Trinity is there. I have a choice. We all have a choice. I choose dancing, joy, gratitude, and fierce grace.

Chapter 12

Flow

It flows.

Trickle, bubble, gurgle.

Out of the ground it comes,

Life must start somewhere.

Flow, swirl, slide.

Running and darting, dodging and slowing to sleep.

Energized by simply existing

Bits and pieces flowing in

Adding to the beauty and grace of our beings.

Chapter 13

Epilogue

I was recently at a creative retreat called *Spark* in Northern Ireland. One of the main topics of the retreat was self-sabotage. In the first main session, a participant mentioned that she was afraid to write because she didn't want to look back on her writing and be ashamed of it or find it unrepresentative of who she was going to be in the future. She wondered how to get past this issue. It was interesting to hear someone ask this question out loud. I'm not sure I would have been able to voice such a fear.

But as I've written and explored my spiritual journey through writing this book, I have been repeatedly reminded that nothing in my life has gone to waste, and it's been a beautiful (if terrifying and painful) journey. The person that I was in elementary, middle, and high school, college, and my twenties or thirties was a beautiful person and is allowed to be who she was at the time. Like the heart orb that Suitcase and I hung up to bring joy to people who stayed in the guestroom of Wisdom's farmhouse, our old selves sparkle and shine in ways that remind us of the beauty of the journey. They remind us that fierce grace is always at work, especially when we least expect it.

I think the most important lesson fierce grace taught me this year is that I am enough. I am reminded of my discernment in April around going to Northern

Ireland, and the comments my peer group had for me. They are the ones who told me that I was enough, that my worry about spending a couple thousand dollars to then be disappointed by not getting any meaningful content was unfounded because what I bring to the experience is the value. They told me that whatever happens, I am enough. I didn't believe them at the time, but I implicitly trust them so I signed up and went. Surprisingly, I realized that this idea of being enough had become somewhat embodied in me during the previous six months. I was sitting at the retreat the first day, being asked what I expected to get out of the five days. I honestly didn't have an answer other than "nothing." I wasn't there to get something, I was there to be and experience community, scenery, and space. I was there to be present to what is. Granted, I'm not even remotely always present, but I wasn't searching for something to make me better or unlock some mystery within me for additional transformation. I was there to notice, to be present, and to live into being enough regardless of what the content was during the retreat. I am enough. All of me, the ugly and beauty and everything in between, is enough.

As I've entered life again after traveling, I have noticed that most people don't live from this place of enough-ness. It's been a long transformation for me but now that I'm living into it, life is so much less stressful. Enough-ness is a much more life-giving place to live from. This is not surprising, I realize. Many, many ideas, false beliefs, and habits have had to be shed over the last eleven years in order to get here. And I'm not even close to finished yet because fierce grace doesn't stop. There's always another invitation, even if it's simply to revel in the beauty and wonder of what is at the present moment. Revel, we get to revel.

Maybe that's what Jesus did when he walked the earth, he reveled in the messy beauty of his creation, including himself. He experienced his new physicality in a way that was extravagant, unnecessary, and probably undignified. My spiritual director asked me once if I thought Jesus got diarrhea. At that point I hadn't thought about it and after the initial shock of the question, I hedged my bets on yes. Just like Jesus probably got blisters from his sandals, stepped in sheep poop, and smelled bad after traveling between cities. He was human and chose to be human, which means that Jesus chose to experience all that it means to be human. Love, loss, anger, pain, joy, compassion, death, and elation were part of the deal. They aren't things to which we are to hold tightly, but we're invited to experience and cherish as long as they bring life, knowing when to leave them behind or let them fall away.

And that's the stuff right there, the stuff of enough-ness and fierce grace: to revel, to experience, to let go, to be enough.

As I've learned again this year, being protected shouldn't be my highest priority, struggle can be somewhat overrated, and drama can be a form of self-sabotage. I am enough (say it with me, "I am enough!") and don't need external approval or gratification to be in a deep and loving relationship with myself, Trinity, Wisdom, and the world. Jesus being with me through the pain, joy, happiness and tears is enough. Fierce grace is enough.

Acknowledgements

My heartfelt appreciation goes to Marybeth Morrison, Andi Cumbo-Floyd, Marcus Mills, Brent Salsgiver, and Mark Messner for their assistance, critique, and guidance in various forms throughout this process. I am indebted to Missy Schoonover for her patience, sense of humor, and comradery as I finally wrote the book she has been encouraging me to write for years. I am grateful for my husband, Pat, who encouraged me to pursue writing in spite of my excellent objections.

I'd also like to thank Ed Cyzewski for developmental and copy editing, Lisa Delay for her cover design, and Katherine Sleadd for her photography work.

Finally, to "Mindy" and "Bill," I would not be who I am without your input, persistence, honesty, and grace. Thank you for holding space for me to encounter and respond to fierce grace.

Made in the USA
Middletown, DE
14 July 2019